The Reliant Motor Company

Elvis Payne

NOSTALGIA ROAD

First published by Crécy Publishing Ltd 2016

A CIP record for this book is available from the British Library

ISBN 9781908 347367

Printed in Slovenia by GPS Group

**Nostalgia Road is an imprint of
Crécy Publishing Limited**
1a Ringway Trading Estate
Shadowmoss Road
Manchester M22 5LH
www.crecy.co.uk

All images are from author's collection unless otherwise stated. All images marked RSSOC are from the Reliant Sabre & Scimitar Owners Club.

Front main:
The Scimitar GTE SE5 offered the world something that had not been available before; a sporting estate car.

Front inset left to right:
The Robin 850 not only boasted, as the name suggest, a more powerful 848cc engine but also a number of more subtle changes like a revised grille that consisted of three chrome bars.

The Rebel claimed the title of being the first model from a new manufacturer to enter the British family car market since before World War 2.

Despite the Bond name, the Bond Bug was all Reliant and aimed at the 17 to 25 age group.

Back clockwise from bottom right:
With a large single opening rear door, the Kitten estate was an ideal car for visiting the seaside.

With no doors, access to the Bond Bug was via an upward opening canopy, as it was envisaged that youthful drivers and passengers would be scrambling in and out through the large openings on either side. *Ron Biggin*

Registered in January 1984, FOH 274V was the second Scimitar SS1 prototype built.

Project R931's proposed new baby Scimitar sports car.

Reliant 8cwt vans on the assembly line in 1948 at the time so many orders were being placed, production could not keep up resulting in a three-month waiting list.

Both the 10cwt open truck and 10cwt van now featured a fuel filler at the side of the body with the petrol tank being repositioned under the body on the right-hand side.

Unlike the 7cwt model that used chains to drive a semi-floating rear axle, the 10cwt utilised a more conventional car-type propeller shaft to drive a spiral-bevel rear axle.

The author's ex-1972 Supervan III 5cwt van (Ole Blue) seen here during a photoshoot for a classic car magazine.

CONTENTS

Princess Anne at Reliant on 15th July 1975.

Foreword

It started with the OGLE GTS that was lent to my Father after the 1965 Motor Show, which became the Reliant Scimitar GTE that I eventually came to own and become a Scimitar owner of many years standing. I have long admired the marque and remember touring the Reliant factory in July 1975 when the company was at its peak.

I am pleased that Mr. Payne has taken the time and effort to write this book as this is the first book that covers all Reliant vehicles, both three and four wheels, in a single volume. As the number of Reliants diminish on our roads each year, I am sure this book will give a lot of pleasure to both past and present Reliant owners, recalling as it does the Company's history.

BUCKINGHAM PALACE

The founders of Reliant, E S Thompson (on the left) and T L Williams who both built the original prototype in 1934. They are seen here in 1962.

Introduction

The Reliant Motor Company is perhaps one of the most underrated car manufacturers in the world, If you stopped someone in the street and asked them what they know about Reliant you would perhaps get one of three responses: 'They made the Reliant Robin', often misquoted as a 'Robin Reliant'; 'They made the Reliant Scimitar'; and, 'Didn't Princess Anne own one?' Surprisingly little, for a company that spanned 66 years and achieved so much. The world of Reliant, therefore, is often a mystery to many people with perhaps just enthusiasts of the company's vehicles and ex-employees knowing the full picture. Reliant may have just been a relatively small motor company positioned on the A5 in Tamworth, Staffordshire, though that company served numerous businesses and brought family motoring to the masses with its three-wheelers. It innovated, achieving many world firsts; it exported vehicles all over the world; and, it created a complete car industry for Israel and Turkey. Its Scimitar GTE was emulated one way or another by almost every other car manufacturer and became the choice of royalty and numerous celebrities. These points alone are just the tip of the iceberg and, to cover every vehicle Reliant made in full detail, would take several volumes. Therefore, the aim of this book is to be the first book that provides an in-depth overview of Reliant's history in a single volume that includes both three- and four-wheel models. The book also banishes a few of the myths that have appeared over the last few years and increasingly appear to be accepted as historical facts. The author admits he has also not been immune to these myths with past publications and so this book has gone back to the basics, researching from scratch and involving as many people as possible who were at Reliant at the time.

My own interest in Reliant dates back to 1990, when prior to going to university, my motorcycle (a 1979 Yamaha XS250) was stolen and my mum suggested that I buy a Reliant Robin. This, she said, could be fully loaded with my luggage whilst travelling to and from university and, more importantly, could be driven on a motorcycle licence. It was buying a 1974 Reliant Robin that created a spark for all things Reliant leading on to a number of other three wheeled Reliants over the years. Strangely, all my Reliants have also had names (where as my motorcycles and four-wheeled cars have not) with my first Robin being nicknamed *Gwen*. My other Reliants have also included a 1972 Supervan III (*Ole Blue*) that, in my ownership, was fully restored from the ground up and a 1961 Regal Mk VI van (*Lucie*) that, with its 747cc side-valve engine, enjoyed several appearances on the small screen. Whilst at university I was also fortunate enough to base one of my projects on Reliant, which resulted in a personal tour of Reliant in April 1993 to gain more information. At that point in time the company was making just 25 Robins and three Scimitar Sabres a week. My interest also lead to the creation of my website at www.3-wheelers.com in 2000 which was followed more recently with www.reliant.website a website dedicated for all things Reliant.

This book is arranged in chronological order, though having several models in production at the same time might have led to the book jumping all over the place. As a result, the history of each model is detailed as a whole with the next section of the book reverting back to the next event/model.

Elvis Payne
Tamworth, January 2016

The first Regal production car at Reliant with E.S.Thompson (far left) and his daughter, Pat (far right) in 1952. *Pat Afford*

Acknowledgements

First of all I would like to express my gratitude to HRH The Princess Royal for agreeing to provide a foreword for this book. Her interest in and knowledge of the company go back to when she first acquired a Scimitar.

My sincere thanks go to Barrie Wills (former deputy Managing Director at Reliant), for not only the wealth of information provided via numerous emails but also for painstakingly proof reading this entire book and offering advice. Writing this book would have been a much harder task if it was not for Dave Poole, Kerry Croxton and Thomas Touw, who all went above and beyond providing numerous bits of information, photographs and scans of the *Reliant Review*. Thanks are also due to the following people who have assisted directly or indirectly with either information, photographs and proof reading: Alan Gold, Andy Plumb, Anne Sullivan, Barry Mansfield-Stokes, Bob Neale, Brian Marshall, Carl Langridge, Clive Stanley, Dave Corby, David Yando, Derrick Smith, Edward Osmond, Gill Richardson (and everyone at Crécy Publishing), Ian McLoughlin, Jacky Phillips, Joe Mason, John Copestake, John Tracey, John Wilson-Hall, Jonathan Heynes, Karen Bailey, Kate Pointon, Kevin Leech, Les Collier, Les Turner, Leslie Gobbett, Lol French, Malcolm Dennis, Mark and Sue Cropper, Marian Whitefoot, Marlene Gaskin, Martin Strange, Matt Greenly, Maureen Plant, Maurice and Jill Wilson, Mike Hyatt, Onur Selçuk, Pamela Wilson, Pat Afford (acknowledging E S Thompson & Colin Fine-Thompson), Paul Brown, Penny Baxter, Mick Riley (and members of the Tamworth & Warwickshire Facebook group), Peter Stevens, Photo Storch, Raymond Whitehurst, Reliant Owners Club, Reliant Sabre & Scimitar Owners Club, Robert Pickett, Ron Biggin, Ruth Kitchen (acknowledging Ray Wiggin), Simon Drake, Stewart Halstead, Stuart Cyphus, Sverker P Zethelius, *Tamworth Herald*, Tamworth Library, Tom Karen, Winifred Mortimer and last but no means least my wife, Caroline, for her continued support and our son, Harvey, for constantly enriching our lives.

One man and his plan

Born at 43 Church Street in Tamworth in May 1890, Tom Lawrence Williams was the seventh child of seven children. Excelling at school, he went on to become a civil engineer for Nuneaton Council and it was the start of World War 1 that possibly set up a path that would ultimately lead him into creating one of the largest British-owned car manufacturing companies. As a Christadelphian by faith, Williams was not willing to fight and so, as a conscientious objector, he was summoned to court on 30 March 1916 charged with being an absentee from his Majesty's Army. Due to Williams' background as a civil engineer his skills were in demand and so he escaped imprisonment, was fined the minimum of £2 and handed over to military custody. Undertaking work of national importance led Williams to working for companies like Dunelt, Triumph and then the Raleigh Cycle Company in Nottingham in 1931 as chief designer in the motor vehicles department.

Tom Williams (far right) at Raleigh in the early 1930s.

As Chief Designer at Raleigh, Tom Williams was responsible for much of the design for Raleigh Safety Seven introduced in 1933. *Martin Strange*

Famous for its bicycles, Raleigh, like most other bicycle companies at the time, ventured into the world of motorised vehicles manufacturing motorcycles alongside its bicycles. It had tried this many years earlier in 1903, creating the three-wheel Raleighette, though abandoned production of it in 1906 and returned to building bicycles and motorcycles before then also dropping its motorcycle range. In 1929, it decided to try again by acquiring the rights to the Ivy Karryal van, building its own version that was essentially a 500cc motorcycle with a third wheel and an enclosed 5cwt van body. The Raleigh LDV (Light Delivery Van) made no attempt to hide its motorcycle ancestry with its exposed front wheel, girder forks, handlebar steering and an angular box body for the load area, whilst the driver's cab consisted of just a windscreen and a roof. In 1931 the engine was boosted to 600cc though it remained a single-seater until 1933, when a two-passenger version was introduced.

Tom Williams was responsible for much of the appearance, mechanics and layout of the LDV as well as the Raleigh Safety Seven that followed in 1933. The Safety Seven was a new three-wheel passenger vehicle, which as the name implied, was powered by an 7bhp, air cooled 742cc, V-twin engine that was designed and manufactured by Raleigh. Although the LDV was utilitarian in its appearance with its exposed front end, the Safety Seven featured a full aluminium body fastened onto an ash framework that covered the front wheel, presenting a much more car-like appearance. Despite the LDV van finding a small niche in the market, the directors at Raleigh were not so convinced and became restless. Not really seeing a future for the vehicles they soon decided to cease manufacturing motor vehicles altogether and concentrate solely on building bicycles.

Williams however disagreed with their views and firmly believed that there was a major market for a smaller van amongst general tradesmen and small companies, where a motorcycle and box-sidecar were too small and vehicles over 8cwt were too large. Williams' belief was so strong that he decided to prove Raleigh wrong and resigned from the company determined that he would build his own vehicles.

Reliant Prototype

At the time Williams lived with his in-laws at Bro-Dawel in Kettlebrook, Tamworth and set about creating a workshop in their back garden. After securing a loan from Barclays Bank, Williams started work on the Reliant prototype in August 1934, and from October 1934, was assisted by former Raleigh spares shop manager, E S ('Tommo') Thompson, who resigned from Raleigh at the same time. Thompson believed in Williams' views, and together, the pair created their version of a small three-wheel delivery van.

Naturally, having both been associated with the Raleigh LDV, their new vehicle showed many similarities. However, whilst they were able to machine parts for it at Tamworth Motor Garage in Aldergate, Tamworth, Williams and Thompson were mainly confined to household hand tools and so it was not as finely finished as the Raleigh. Their three wheeler was very basic with a box body consisting of a hardwood frame and metal panels, no rear suspension, handlebar steering, exposed motorcycle type front forks and was fitted with a 600cc JAP (J A Prestwich Ltd) single-cylinder air-cooled engine. Once the vehicle was completed, it was then that the first major problem arose. As it had been built in Williams' back garden with a width of 4ft 3½in, it was approximately four inches too wide to fit through the gap at the side of the house. The whole thing had to then be dismantled and, as the front driveway had too much of a slope, it was reassembled at Tamworth Motor Garage. Following a photograph published in a 2001 book of a 7cwt pick-up (see page 11) that was incorrectly labelled, it was assumed for a number of years that this was the prototype, although it is now known to be of a 7cwt van that was converted in the 1960s. Furthermore, whilst Williams was testing the prototype van and talking to local traders it seemed apparent that the handlebars were not favoured. Williams did not have the finances to create a second prototype and so the original was modified and the handlebars were substituted for a steering wheel. Other slight modifications were made until Williams was happy that the vehicle was ready to enter production. As many of the parts used had come from Raleigh a number of them were embossed with a capital 'R' and so this dictated what the new three-wheeler would be called. It is said that after looking through the

The Reliant prototype (Reg No RE-8109) seen here in Polesworth whilst being test driven for *The Commercial Motor* magazine in July 1935.
Pat Afford

dictionary 'Reliant' (meaning 'Dependant [on]') was the first word that was deemed suitable for these new vehicles and so the Reliant was born with the prototype Reliant 7cwt being registered with Stafford County Council on 3 January 1935.

After scouting around for premises to build the new vehicle, a 14-year lease was taken on an old disused Midland Red bus depot that was situated on the south side of Watling Street in Two Gates, Tamworth. Having previously been John Thornburn's omnibus garage at the turn of the century, the premises were very old and draughty with leaking ceilings and inadequate facilities. The lease also included the use of the adjoining derelict flourmills that in later life had served as a shoe and boot factory during World War 1. Using skills acquired from his family background as a carpenter, Williams along with Thompson and Reliant's first employee, Baden Powell, set about building wooden offices and a production track and recruited a handful of men so that production of the new Reliant could begin.

Reliant 7cwt

This first vehicle (chassis number 35/5/1), a Reliant 7cwt van was delivered on 3 June 1935. Costing £84 with £4 a year tax, the 7cwt van had a chassis that in a 1936 brochure was described as a:

'Frame constructed in channel steel special side sections, connected by channel cross members and a massive tubular front and centre members, forming a very rigid construction'

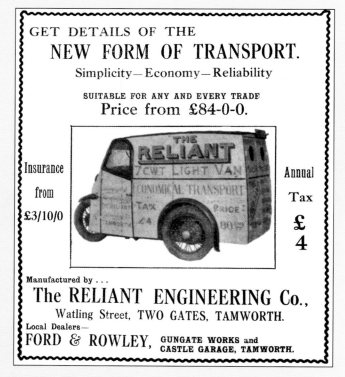

Reliant's first newspaper advertisement appeared in the *Tamworth Herald* on Saturday 6 July 1935.

The 7cwt van boasted two doors to the cab, safety glass, electric lighting set, windscreen wiper and detachable side screens.

Registered on 11 January 1936, this particular 7cwt van was more than likely manufactured in late 1935 and thus one of few early surviving vans. Externally the 7cwt is identified with running lights attached to the side of the body rather than at the front as on all other models.

It was fitted with box body made from aluminium panels that were attached to an ash frame except for the side panels and rear doors that were made from a 'special anti-drum weather resisting material'. Just behind and either side of the steering wheel were two 3½-gallon fuel tanks. The steering wheel itself was positioned centrally within the body with the driver sitting astride the engine, the seat needing to be lifted to start it via a foot pedal starter. The engine was a single cylinder 6bhp (600cc) JAP, air-cooled, side-valve engine that developed 15bhp. It drove the rear axle by chain via a Burman three-speed and reverse gearbox and provided a top speed of 40mph (64km/h), though this was said to be drastically reduced to 5-8mph (8-13km/h) when fully loaded on a steep hill. Thankfully, the driver was always aware of this as the speedometer was detailed as being included in the price. In addition to the van version, a 7cwt open truck (pick-up) version was also created for the same price. This had a swing-down tailboard and an optional extra of a ladder carrying bracket for £3 3s 0d extra.

The Reliant Engineering Company (Tamworth) Ltd was registered on 3 August 1935 with Williams as Managing Director and Thompson (described as a true 'fag-packet draughtsman' by those who knew him on account of always drawing designs on the back of cigarette packets) as Works Manager. The new company was divided into 5,000 ordinary shares of one pound (£1) each and in the same month Walter Halland, Henry (O S) Bridcutt, John Ford, and John Rowley were signed in as directors of the company. Both Ford and Rowley

Right from the start, Reliant also built custom bodies, if required, tailored for a customer's personal requirements as with this converted 7cwt van. The white halo is Reliant's technique for painting around the vehicle to lift it from the photo for advertising purposes. *Thomas Touw*

The 1936 7cwt open truck was designed for the building trade, billposters and market gardeners and listed a ladder-carrying bracket as an optional extra.

The JAP 600cc, single-cylinder, air-cooled engine was used to power the 7cwt Reliant from 1935 to 1938.

were already agents for Hillman, Standard, Wolseley and Rover cars and owned joint garages with the Ford and Rowley Garage in Upper Gungate, Tamworth, and the Castle Garage in Ladybank, Tamworth and so they also became Reliant's first main dealer.

Long believed to be a photo of the prototype, this photo actually dates from around 1971 and showed what was believed, at the time, to be the sole survivor of the first batch of 1935 Reliant vans. It was converted to a pick up in the 1960s and fitted with a BSA Bantam engine and was used on a smallholding for moving soil.

The Reliant Engineering Company (Tamworth) Ltd, company number 303788, was officially registered on 3 August 1935.

11

Largely due to its lack of power and partly due to its load area, the Reliant 7cwt struggled to find buyers and the fledgling company faced the real possibility of bankruptcy having barely got off the ground. Thankfully the old bus premises were fitted with two 1,000-gallon fuel tanks under the building and, after purchasing two petrol pumps, Reliant supplemented its income selling petrol. By the end of 1935, with just 105 vehicles built, the future was not looking promising, especially as the workers could not be paid their wages. Having only been on the board as a director for just over three months Bridcutt resigned from his position. Williams knew now more than ever that for the company to succeed a larger more car-like model was required.

Reliant 10cwt

Wasting no time, a new model was planned to be built alongside the 7cwt and, in March 1936 a larger 10cwt model was introduced with a retail price of £106 10s. Although the 10cwt had a slightly longer wheelbase and wider body, outwardly both models were very similar in appearance but quite different underneath. Powered by a larger, 747cc V-twin water-cooled JAP industrial engine, the new Reliant drove the rear axle by a shaft instead of a chain as in its predecessor and had three forward gears and a reverse. The interior saw the driver seated on the right-hand side (instead of in the centre) and the dual fuel tanks were replaced with a tank under the body and a filler cap on the right-hand side of the vehicle. There was also the option of a starter motor that meant, if fitted, the driver did not need to lift up the seat to start the engine. As the floor space at Reliant was so tight a deal was struck with the Plough & Harrow public house in Fazeley to use its outbuildings and, as a result, the wooden frames were built there and then carried by hand four-tenths of a mile (0.64km) to the main factory.

Reliant soon found a market with various companies; these newly built 10cwt vehicles were bound for LMS Express — the London, Midlands & Scottish Railway parcel delivery service. *Pat Afford*

The cover of a 1936 Reliant brochure showing the 10cwt van. The brochure covers the JAP-powered models and is part of the author's collection. To date, it is the only known surviving copy.

The first 10cwt was delivered on 26 March 1936, and it soon became the commercial success that the company desperately needed. By the end of 1937 Reliant was building 10 vehicles a week compared with five a week a year earlier. Realising that the market for the 10cwt was greater than that of the 7cwt, Williams had been exploring how the vehicles could be improved further, believing that they needed to be more car-like and dispose of the motorcycle-type engine. In October 1937, Williams struck a deal with the Austin Motor Co, which would supply Reliant with the water-cooled, four-cylinder, side-valve, 747cc engine and gearbox from the Austin Seven. However, before the JAP powered models were phased out, the last 23 models were special versions fitted with a 747cc air-cooled engine.

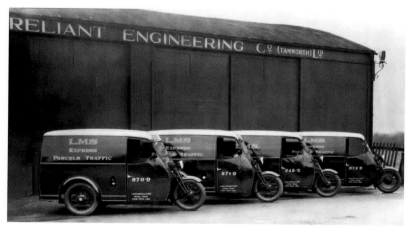

Along with its JAP engine the 7cwt model featured a three-speed gearbox, patented springing system and inter-changeable wheels. Also note the twin petrol tanks, one either side of the steering wheel.

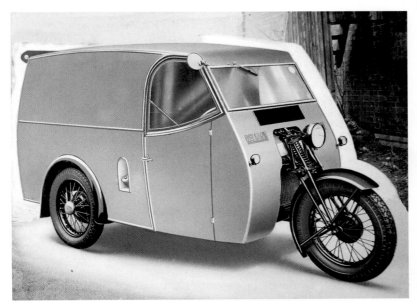

The 10cwt van was a great success and convinced Williams that there was a market for a van with a larger loading capacity.

Reliant 8cwt/12cwt

A new 8cwt Austin-powered Reliant was announced in March 1938, just two months after the JAP-powered 7cwt and 10cwt models had been discontinued. This in turn was joined four months later by a slightly larger model in the form of the 12cwt. Williams' persistence in maintaining a car-like three-wheeler had paid off and towards the end of 1938 sales were going well, with not only small companies buying them but railway companies and many of the large stores in London and the provincial areas. Reliant had also entered the export market, shipping vehicles to South Africa, Australia, South America and India. For export orders the vehicles were often shipped minus their bodywork as these were then custom built the other side. The company now employed 50 men and at its peak was producing at least 25 vehicles a week. Just as it seemed everything was at last on track, Austin announced that the Austin Seven range was to cease manufacture in 1939. In turn, this meant the engine would no longer be available. This was quite a predicament for Williams as his vans were now, to all intents and purposes, real cars on three wheels and especially, given how the Austin engine had performed, he did not want to go backwards to a motorcycle-type engine. As there were no other small light car engines on the market, Williams, as a mechanic did the only thing he could do, and that was to decide that Reliant would design and build its own engine.

Above: Both the 10cwt open truck and 10cwt van now featured a fuel filler at the side of the body with the petrol tank being repositioned under the body on the right-hand side.

Right: The 747cc twin-cylinder, water-cooled, JAP engine with a three-speed and reverse gearbox was used in the 10cwt van from 1936 to 1938.

Below: Unlike the 7cwt model that used chains to drive a semi-floating rear axle, the 10cwt utilised a more conventional car-type propeller shaft to drive a spiral-bevel rear axle.

Introduced in 1938, the 8cwt van was powered by a 7bhp Austin Seven engine.

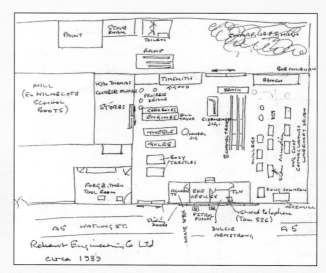

Drawn by E S Thompson (marked EST), this plan circa 1939, shows just how compact Reliant was in its early days in the old Midland Red Bus garage. Also present are the petrol pumps on the forecourt and a single shared telephone (No 336) that was in TLW (Williams) office. *Pat Afford*

Reliant's first engine

In designing the new engine, to help save development and production cost, Williams and Thompson leaned very heavily on the Austin unit, emulating it as far as they could. As a result they produced an engine that was almost identical, with a water-cooled 747cc four-cylinder side-valve unit that had a detachable cast-iron head and a cast-iron cylinder block mounted on an aluminium crankcase. The engine, though, was different as they repositioned the distributor mounting on the cylinder head and changed several important internal dimensions from the original Austin blueprint. This meant that a number of components were not interchangeable between the two types of engine. This was a tactical move that not only allowed them to improve slightly on the engine but also to ensure customers would return to them for spare parts rather than go to Austin agents.

The Reliant four-cylinder, side-valve engine with Solex carburettor and three-speed plus reverse gearbox with Borg & Beck clutch.

With supply of the Austin engine exhausted, the new Reliant engine was developed at such a pace that on 3 September 1939 the first all-Reliant engine burst into life on the test bench. However, its burbling exhaust note was joined with news on the radio that the country was now at war. Just a month later the new engine was being fitted in production to both the 8cwt and 12cwt models with the 7.5bhp unit producing a maximum of 14bhp at 3,500rpm. In the same year Reliant purchased the site on which it was based by taking advantage of a clause in the lease contract to acquire the site. Now the company was the holder of the freehold, it started to expand the buildings by creating a new body shop.

The War Years

Reliant began its war work on 11 September 1939 when a consignment of 13,200 civilian respirators arrived at the factory at 11am in the morning. Williams had volunteered the assistance of a team of 30 staff members in assembling the mask that were designated for the general public. Working until 11pm at night, the staff assembled 11,000 respirators with the remaining being completed the next day. These were then passed on to newly formed village respirator depots where they were handed over to Air Raid wardens who visited each household within the area distributing the masks.

The National Emergency leading up to World War 2 continued to escalate and, by January 1940, along with the introduction of food rationing, the production of motor vehicles had been suspended with just 80 Reliant vans being built with the new Reliant engine. The doors at Reliant, however, remained open although the company instantly lost half of its floor space when it was requisitioned by the government for the nut and bolt manufacturer, L H Newton & Co Ltd.

Instead of building three-wheelers, workers were now producing items for the war effort. At times they had no idea what they were making and were just told to follow the blue prints and remember, 'Careless talk cost lives'. On the opposite side of the road to the Reliant Engineering Co was a row of 14 terrace houses known as Park Place. At least seven of these houses had cellars and, as the buildings at Reliant offered no protection against falling bombs should an air raid occur, employees would evacuate the building and seek protection in the houses. Pamela Wilson, whose parents lived opposite Reliant in Park Place during the war, remembers her dad telling her about this saying:

'...when the war was on the workers from Reliant used to come and use our cellars in the air raids. Mum use to get a bit concerned at times in case anyone accidentally sat on your brother who was a tiny baby and was laying in the chair.'

Reliant also helped to support the local area and often donated generously to local causes with Williams occasionally matching amounts raised by his staff. One such beneficiary was the 'Tamworth & District Spitfire Fund'. In October 1940 the staff and employees had raised £29 9s with Williams then matching the amount raised and providing an additional donation.

Although the company was doing its bit for the war effort, it was not immune from its laws and often found itself on the wrong side of them during a black out. The first reported instance was on 13 September 1940 when P W R Hull was passing the factory at 10:45pm at night and saw the building of a wall lit up by a red glow. Upon investigation he found a pile of rubbish on fire with flames four to five feet high which lit up the whole yard. A local neighbour, Mrs Maud Grice, provided water to extinguish the fire and later proclaimed, 'It was a jolly good fire'. Both Williams and Thompson stated that the fire had been burning for four days and that it must have reignited itself as there was no glow from it two hours earlier. The company was fined £2 10s and 15s special costs.

Similar instances were to recur throughout the war with electric lights being left on. One such example was on 28 November 1941 when Kenneth Mather (a machine turner at Reliant) left the light on to the bicycle sheds. Reliant had actually painted external light bulbs so they provided a dimmer light though in this instance the paint had started to peel off. The light, a 60W bulb, was spotted on the roadside by Special Constable Lunn. Despite Thompson contending

Reliant spent the war years machining parts for the various ministries. This advertisement is from the *Tamworth Herald* of 30 March 1940.

that the light was so faint the Constable could not read his own writing on his note pad and that it was not sufficiently bright enough to assist enemy aircraft both Mather and Reliant were fined £1 each with an additional £1 for special cost.

Despite these lighting issues, Reliant was totally committed in assisting the war effort and, during the course of World War 2, it produced around 1,500,000 parts. In September 1945, an exhibition was held at the Town Hall in Tamworth in connection with the National Savings Thanksgiving Week and, amongst other things, local companies displayed items they made as part of the war effort. The *Tamworth Herald* on Saturday 20 October 1945 stated of Reliant (and also L H Newton & Co who occupied half of their floor space):

> 'Take the stand of the Reliant Engineering Co., Ltd. for an example. Bits and pieces — it was difficult in their separate entities to visualise what part they played, but the labels told the story. This was a bit of a Lancaster bomber, that was a piece for a Churchill tank. All the famous aircraft and tank names seemed to be there, and there were bits and pieces for jeeps and armoured cars and other jobs as well .... Even lower in the scale of size were some of the parts shown by Messrs. L. H. Newton & Co., Ltd. the vital bits and pieces here ranging down to a pin-head smallness, yet each was a perfect specimen of its kind.'

Like many companies throughout the country, Reliant also lost a number of their employees to the war whilst Williams also suffered his own personal loss when his wife Ellen died, following a long-term illness, in November 1940.

Following World War 2, the ban on vehicle production was lifted in 1946 and so Reliant returned to three-wheeler production with manufacture of the 8cwt recommencing in June 1946. Reliant had now become one of Tamworth's key employers taking on more people to help meet demand, especially ex-servicemen. One such employee was Tom H Scott, who had just been demobilised from the RAF and was offered a job in the Sales Department in the same month. Several months later, in February 1947, the 12cwt model also resumed production with both models built along the same guidelines as their pre-war counterparts and powered by the Reliant 747cc engine. With reference to the engine, an Owners' Instruction Book for the 8 and 12cwt van in the same year details:

> 'With the advent of war in 1939, early teething troubles had been overcome and production of the new engine is well in hand. Its complete reliability was subsequently proven under the exacting war conditions that followed, and we feel we can justify claim to have produced an engine fully in keeping with Reliant tradition and quality.'

Export or Die

The war had a devastating effect on the British economy and, as a result, the United Kingdom was financially destitute. In order to bring money back into the country the government decreed that all manufacturers should sell their goods abroad. The phrase 'Export or Die', first coined by Hans Juda for *The Ambassador* magazine became the motto of the time and British car makers started to ship vehicles abroad in their thousands. Numerous orders poured into Reliant and the company was now working flat out to try and keep up with demand. From order to delivery (on domestic orders), an 8cwt model was taking approximately three months, whilst those ordering a 12cwt model had to wait at least six to nine months for delivery. To make things worse conditions were severely cramped as L H Newton & Co still occupied half of the floor space that had been requisitioned for them during the war and Reliant had often to overcome difficulties in sourcing materials such as bearings, tubing and even wood for making the frames.

For export orders, though, it was a completely different story as they took priority. This was demonstrated in April 1948 when an overseas order to Melbourne, Australia for six 12cwt vans took less than three weeks to process. The history of the Australia shipment actually dated back to 1934 when the Raleigh Cycle Co exported the LDV van there. Once Raleigh ceased manufacturing the vehicles, Williams then seized the opportunity to supply them with Reliant vans instead. Whereas early vehicles were exported with no bodywork, production difficulties in Australia resulted in the dealers asking for complete vans. To help reduce the landing charges at the docks, the vehicles were shipped in SKD (semi-knocked down) form with the bodies being boxed up in parts with detailed instructions and photographs showing how they should be re-assembled being sent to Melbourne in advance by air-mail. Reliant was also machining and exporting parts, including diesel engine components, mining equipment and automobile parts for a number of companies. One major customer was Rootes Securities, which at the time were makers of the Hillman Minx.

Reliant had a long association with the Rootes group and, in dealing with the company, Williams met Leonard Engledow with whom he struck up an instant rapport. Engledow was part of the senior management for Rootes and Williams approached him offering the job as General Manager at Reliant. Engledow accepted, joining the company in September 1947 and shortly afterwards also became a director. Although Reliant had been building vehicles since 1935, there were no specific part numbers for all the components used to build a van and, thus, no two Reliants were truly identical. Workers often used different parts that they called by different names that did the job rather than the actual part. One of the first fruits of Engledow's employment

Whether as kits or complete vehicles, Reliant found soon success in exporting its vehicles around the globe. This particular one was a Reliant Rickshaw built upon an 8cwt van chassis.

Although poor quality, this image from April 1948 captures six semi-knocked down Reliant 12cwt vans, boxed up in a number of wooden crates labelled 'Footscay, Melbourne' and bound for the docks to be hoisted aboard the SS *Soudan*. *Tamworth Herald*

was the appointment of 24-year-old John Tracey in July 1948. Tracey was assigned the task of not only procuring parts but also cataloguing and providing all parts with specific part numbers and a generic name. Within six months the task was done and all parts had unique identifiers. This helped create a range of vehicles that were not only a lot more uniform in their construction but also assisted customers and dealers identify and request spare parts more easily.

In 1948, Williams, along with Thompson and Engledow, approached the Morson Engineering Co in Coventry, a company that manufactured gears. Williams had long believed in the philosophy: 'why should we pay someone else to do something we can do ourselves?' They recognised the benefits if Reliant could cut its own gears. A deal was struck and Reliant acquired Morson Engineering; this also bought along with it the skills of their director, Tommy Law, who then assisted Reliant in teaching the company how to build its own gearbox and also how to further improve its engine.

David Peckover, Plumber, Domestic & Sanitary Engineer and Gas Fitter of Bradford was one of the many small companies that found a use for the 8cwt van, this one being a 1949 model.

Reliant 8cwt vans on the assembly line in 1948; at the time so many orders were being placed, production could not keep up resulting in a three-month waiting list.

Regent

In an attempt to keep up with demand, the workforce was now split into day and night shifts. As production increased so did the factory space as Reliant extended its buildings further and also built a new wood compound. This meant frames could now be machined on site.

The post-war boom in vehicle production had brought numerous models from other car manufacturers, many with exotic shapes compared with their pre-war counterparts. The Reliant, however, still followed its tried and tested design, where functionality and practicality were more important than good looks. In an effort to change its styling, small windows were added behind the doors of both models in March 1949.

In an attempt to update the appearance of its vans further in March 1950, the company replaced its 12cwt by the new Reliant 10cwt Regent. The body of the Regent had been extensively redesigned by Ron Taylor at Reliant with a much squarer appearance, whilst an open backed pick-up version was also reintroduced. It again consisted of metal panels attached to a seasoned ash frame and a Rexine-covered roof. The doors had been widened and included sliding safety glass windows whilst inside a new steel dashboard was fitted. The lines of the body were enhanced further with new pressed steel, 'easi-clean' wheels that were complemented with heavily chromed Nave plates. Whilst outwardly this seemed like a new vehicle, under the skin the basic chassis layout and engine were the same as its predecessor though unlike other 'girder fork' type Reliants, the 10cwt Regent was the only one to be equipped with a 12V electrical system.

With a larger, squarer body the 10cwt Regent had a body capacity of 106cu ft and a payload of 1,120lb (509kg).

Whilst the Regent 10cwt weighed (as Reliant quoted it) 'approx.1,008lbs unladen' it fell into a higher tax bracket of £10 a year as essentially it was too heavy to be classed as a tricycle. It was, therefore, complemented by a smaller brother, with the 8cwt van continuing in production alongside it. Initially with the exception of the quoted payload being reduced to 6cwt the physical appearance remained the same though with a weight of 'approx. 882lbs unladen' the new 6cwt weight only attracted £5 a year tax. As with the 12cwt models before it, the Regent was also exported abroad in a SKD format to various countries, including Czechoslovakia and Israel.

At the same time as the Regent was launched, Reliant also announced a new redesigned engine that had a longer life. Led by Fred Hollister, a number of changes were made to the original unit; these included force feeding oil to the crankshaft bearings by a submerged gear pump (replacing a splash system with a vane-type pump), replacing steel-back white metal bearings for ball and roller bearings, an improved crankshaft connecting-rod along with fully floating gudgeon pins and flange fixing for the flywheel. Such were the changes to the engine that Williams described it as a 'new engine' and new piecework rates were fixed in the engine department. These

Above: As with its predecessors, the Regent was a firm favourite with many businesses; this one was used by the London Co-operative Society. *Thomas Touw*

Left: A Regent 10cwt chassis with long semi-elliptic undersprung rear springs, Girling brakes and Burman Douglas steering.

were not well received by those assembling the engine and a dispute soon arose. Unable to find an agreement, on Tuesday afternoon 14 March 1950, over 200 workmen walked out on what became the first strike at Reliant. The following day the workers met early in the morning and decided by ballot to continue the strike until the union representatives had spoken with the management. A follow-up meeting was then held at the Star Inn in Lower Gungate, Tamworth on the same evening. The union, headed by Mr W H Stokes, reported back to the men on his discussions with the management and then later issued a statement acknowledging that they had 'unanimously accepted recommendations put before them'. This meant the strike ended after just two days with an immediate resumption of work on a status quo basis. In addition a small committee of representatives for both sides was set up to look into the question of piecework rates for the 'new engine'.

Introduced in 1950, the 6cwt van was initially identical to the earlier 8cwt model though with a reduced quoted payload. *Paul Brown*

A new 'modern' office block was completed in 1950; it also included a self-contained flat that Tom Williams resided in. *RSSOC*

Over the years whilst the factory area had been growing the actual offices had to a certain degree been overlooked as had the most crucial but less conversational of buildings: the lavatories. In 1949 plans were approved for a new 'modern' office block and better lavatories. The latter also had proper toilet paper as other materials used by the staff were blocking up the toilets. In true Reliant style the new offices (that included a new board room and reception area) were built by Reliant workers under the supervision of Williams and were completed in late 1950 being officially opened on 9 December 1950 by Councillor A Aucot, the Chairman of Tamworth Rural District Council.

Following the death of his first wife, Williams remained at Bro-Dawel in Kettlebrook living with his in-laws though, with the new office expansion, Williams took the opportunity to also have a self-contained flat built above the drawing office that he could reside in. Initially he shared it alongside a Mr and Mrs Chapman, the latter being his housemaid. In the same year Thompson's dedication to the company was rewarded as he became a director whilst also retaining his position as Works Manager.

Whether Reliant had exhausted its supply of wire wheels or whether to upgrade the looks of the 6cwt, in 1951 the model now featured a light make over with pressed steel wheels and cleaner body lines, although it still retained a 6V electrical system. Later in the same year the brakes of all versions were improved as Girling hydraulic dampers were fitted to the front forks. In an effort to upgrade the 6cwt

model further, in September 1952 the 6cwt Prince Regent was introduced; this inherited its styling from the 10cwt Regent model. However, weighing in at 952lb the Prince Regent also fell into the 10cwt tax bracket of £10 a year as it was too heavy to be classed as a tricycle. The original 6cwt model continued to be made alongside; however, despite being advertised to the UK market, it is believed that the Prince Regent may have primarily have been an export model, as the 8cwt limit was not applicable to export models.

The revised 6cwt van featured 'detachable side curtains' and reinforced wire wheels though, on later models, these were changed for 'Easi-clean' pressed steel wheels.

At 980lb the 6cwt Prince Regent was 98lb heavier than the standard 6cwt model and, therefore, too heavy to benefit from a reduced tax rate. As a result few were sold in the UK.

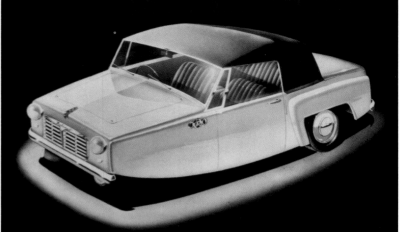

An artist's impression of the Reliant Regal, which, like many impressions of its era, had hyperbolic visual dimensions. The actual production car that followed was much smaller.

The Regal prototype on display at the Earl's Court Motorcycle show in November 1951. *RSSOC*

Regal

Such was the success of Reliant's commercial vans that many owners were converting them into passenger cars by adding seats in the back and additional windows in the side. This was only possible to do after owning a Reliant for several months; to do it too soon would attract the additional Purchase Tax that was added to private cars. Reliant received numerous letters of praise from owners who had converted their vans to homemade saloon cars. At the time, new passenger cars were exceptionally hard to obtain and those that were available could not be driven by many Reliant owners who only had a motorcycle licence. Combined with his own involvement with the Raleigh Safety Seven at the Raleigh Cycle Co, Williams soon realised that the market was crying out for an economical passenger car, though he realised such a passenger car would also bring a number of design challenges with it. Reliant enlisted Allen Bowden, who were industrial designers, and set them the task of producing a new three-wheel passenger car. The designs that then came back were a far cry from the utilitarian style of its commercial vehicles and offered a sleek vehicle that was ahead of its time. Reliant then decided to test the market opinion of such a vehicle and its engineers, along with Ron Taylor who also designed the Regent body, set about building a prototype. As would be expected there were a number of issues, since what works on paper does not necessarily work in real life and

so the body design had to be altered from the original drawings.

Carrying on the theme of Royal model names, the new car was named the Reliant Regal and the prototype was exhibited at the Earl's Court Motorcycle show in November 1951. For its time, the prototype Regal was an impressive-looking motorcar and was a great attraction, though its Achilles' Heel was the projected sale price, calculated at £549 16s 8d including Purchase Tax. Compared with other vehicles at the same show, this was too expensive, especially when its main rival, the Bond Minicar Mk C, was being exhibited a few stands away at only

Reliant's first passenger car — the Regal — with an aluminium body and four seats that offered ample seating for two adults and two small children. The Regal chassis was completely different to the girder fork vans and now used patented torsion bar suspension to the front wheel.

Tom Scott offers information to a line-up of journalists ready to test the Regal at Mount Pleasant, next to the Reliant buildings.

Presented to the National Motor Museum at Beaulieu in September 1973, this particular 1953 Regal was purchased by the Raleigh Safety Seven & Early Reliant Owners Club and restored by Reliant.

£374 3s 4d. It was apparent, therefore, that the design needed to be reconsidered to reduce the cost if it was going to compete in the market place.

To ensure that Reliant was always able to retain a supply of radius arms for the front wheel of the Regal, it purchased Smiths Forgings of Aston, Birmingham in 1952. Rather than be moved in house, Smiths Forgings initially remained in Birmingham and, in addition to the radius arms, the company also produced the camshaft for Reliant engines. In November of the same year, the Regal reappeared at the Motorcycle Show and was far superior to the prototype that had been shown the year before. Although the engine was to remain the same, just about every other part of the design had been altered in some way. To help reduce both the weight and the cost, a number of features, such as wind-down glass windows and exterior door handles, were dropped, helping to bring the price down to £467 7s 10d including Purchase Tax. The Regal was a two-door, four-seat, drop-head coupé, with the body consisting of 18-gauge aluminium panels that were attached to an ash frame. The front had a large bonnet that provided access to a tool kit, radiator and spare wheel. The engine itself was placed so far back in the chassis that access to it was from inside the car by removing a cowl between the front seats. Whilst the body gave the illusion of a rear boot, this was not a boot as such and access to that area also from inside the car by folding down the rear seat. The chassis was also a completely new design, with the two main members made of 18-gauge, box section pressed steel upswept at the rear to clear the rear axle. Where the Regal altered dramatically from previous Reliants was at the front with a single, forged arm linked to a transverse torsion bar suspension system bolted on to a cross member at the front of the chassis, the front wheel being attached to a stub axle on the leading end of the forged arm. This was then all totally enclosed within the body and complemented with single wheel steering mechanism. To steer the wheel, a Burman-Douglas steering box was operated by a drop arm linked to a track rod attached first to a fulcrum on the suspension arm and then by a second track rod to the stub axle steering link. As detailed, the Regal was powered by the 747cc Reliant side-valve engine that was mounted longitudinally behind the front wheel developing 16bhp at 4,000rpm. This drove the rear axle via a propeller shaft through a four-speed non-synchromesh gearbox, which was said to provide a top speed of 65mph (105km/h), whilst being capable of 50mpg (5.6-litre/100km). The Regal, therefore, was not only efficient with its true car like engine but also offered true economy family motoring.

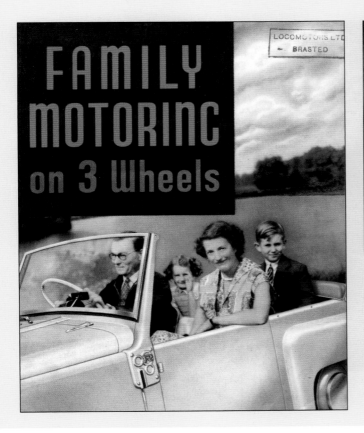

Above: This cross section of the Regal shows just how compact the vehicle was, with the space under the bonnet mainly being taken by both the front wheel and spare wheel.

Left: The first all-colour Reliant brochure was in 1953 and based around the Regal being a car for the family. The Regal offered a new lease of life for many families where the main form of transport had been a motorcycle and sidecar driven on a motorcycle licence.

The *Tamworth Herald* quoted Williams at the time saying:

'I am sure this will be successful – there is a definite demand for a three-wheeler car for the small family man.'

Williams was soon proved to be right as, although the Regal was the most expensive three-wheeler on the market, it quickly established itself as the best regarded available. The contemporary road tests at the time praised it highly for its very complete specification, stating it also had an immediate advantage due to the use of a 'proper' four-cylinder engine compared with the motorcycle-derived units used by many of its competitors.

Davis Divan

Shortly after the Regal went into production, Reliant was contacted by the Delta Motor Car Co in the USA. Formerly the Davis Motor Car Co, the firm started to produce the Davis Divan three-wheeler in the USA from 1947. A year later the company was starting to face issues, as the workers and engineers were not being paid whilst investors and dealers were threatening lawsuits, with over 30 franchisees waiting for delivery of vehicles. It was not long before the plant was

closed down and, in 1950, the company was sold for tax claims. Although 16 vehicles can be accounted for, it is believed that around 18 vehicles were made in total (this figure included a military version). In an attempt to breathe life back into the project, 16 franchise holders, who owned the fifth Davis Divan to be built along with some tooling, then formed the Delta Motor Car Co. Delta contacted Reliant in 1953 and hoped that Reliant would build the car under licence. The fifth Davis Divan (now rebadged as a Delta) was sent to Reliant in 1954 for 'Engineering evaluation'. Robert Pickett, started at Reliant in 1955 and he saw the Davis in that year. Pickett recalls that:

'...they had a Davis Delta American three wheeler in the wood compound in 1955, I reckon you would have got five people in it. I think it was light blue and the workers had it running up and down the A5. I did have the Delta badge off the back, but my stepdad had a clean out and it went missing.'

Reliant concluded their assessment of the Davis in the same year; however, at 15ft long, powered by a 2.3-litre engine and wide enough to seat four adults across, the Davis was much too heavy at 1,111kg to be classed as a tricycle in the UK. It was, therefore, sent to the

The Davis Divan sent to Reliant in 1954 was the fifth vehicle off the production line. Pictured is the fourth vehicle that was made next to it and it still survives in the Lane Motor Museum in the USA.
David Yando

dockyard ready to be shipped back to the USA. The Customs Officers demanded that the customs bond be paid for the car to be sent back to America. At the time the Delta Motor Car Co was not willing /able to pay for return shipment and, as Reliant did not want to pay the customs bond, Reliant was required to 'destroy the car under the eyes of the customs agents'. Delta themselves ran out of funding shortly afterwards and folded, ending any negotiations with Reliant.

Regal Mk II / Regent 10cwt Mk II

Back in the Reliant range, following the success of the Regal, a much improved version, detailed as the Regal Mk II, was introduced in May 1954. Whilst it looked almost identical to the original model, there were a number of subtle alterations to the body; these included an integral windscreen surround that replaced the previously separate frame and the removal of the expensive magnesium alloy front grille to produce a cleaner bodyline. Underneath its skin, the transmission remained the same with the faithful 747cc engine, gearbox and rear axle that were all carried over without modifications.

The Regal Mk II also had an impact on the styling of the Regent van that was still lumbering in the side lines with September 1954 seeing the launch of the Regent 10cwt Mk II. The front end of the vehicle had been completely redesigned and the girder forks exposed

Whilst very similar to the Regal, the most notable difference with the Regal Mk II was the lack of the cast-magnesium grille at the front; this had proved costly to produce.

This glimpse of the Regal Mk II production line shows the model's construction. It used a hardwood frame with aluminium panels then attached to it.

A much younger author test-drives a Regal Mk II in 1991, his first drive in a side-valve model.

The Regent Mk II 10cwt was an attempt to modernise the Regent giving it a new front end based on that of the Regal. *Kerry Croxton*

With a 10cwt load capacity, the Regent Mk II was the last three-wheel van from Reliant to offer such a load space.

The introduction of fibreglass

Whilst producing the Regal, one of Reliant's employees, Ron Taylor, had an interest in a new material known as glass reinforced plastic (GRP) or fibreglass, as it also became known, and he had been testing it. Taylor then introduced the material to Reliant, which then also started to experiment with it. This new material, as its name suggests, consisted of moulded plastic resins infused with finely woven glass matting, and once the chemical reactions involved had taken place, the panels formed could, in some applications, actually be stronger than metal. At the time this was difficult for some to accept, believing that nothing could be stronger than metal itself. Williams and Tom Scott, however, were firm believers and forged ahead, insisting that trials with fibreglass continued.

With Taylor's assistance, the first fruits of Reliant's cautious experiments with fibreglass appeared in 1954 at the Commercial Motor Show, when a new 6cwt van was unveiled. Based on the Regal Mk II chassis that was fitted with stronger rear springs, the 6cwt was built using the traditional method of aluminium panels attached to an ash frame, though it was also fitted with a fibreglass hard top and bonnet that were bonded to the frame. Using the aluminium counterparts to take moulds, Reliant also experimented with other fibreglass sections; these included the dashboard, engine cowling and transmission tunnel. Available in primer only and fitted with just a driver's seat it sold at £353 11s 10d (including Purchase Tax) though, when the vehicle went on sale in January 1955, the payload had been reduced to 5cwt. It is worth noting from this point forward, all Reliant three-wheel vans had a payload of 5cwt and were often referred to by Reliant as simply 'Reliant 5cwt van'. In order to differentiate between the models this book will refer to them by both model name and payload (eg Regal Mk II 5cwt van).

on all previous version were now covered by a foreshortened Regal Mk II-style 'nose'. Despite its new cosmetic make-over, the girder fork van range was really starting to show its age, especially when compared with other manufacturers' vehicles and, in December 1954, the 6cwt models were phased out in favour of a 5cwt capacity van based on the Regal Mk II; this was announced in January 1955. With half of the girder fork range gone and production in full swing on the Regal models, it was only a matter of time before the axe fell on the larger Regent 10cwt models; this occurred in September 1956, bringing to an end a product that, in various forms, had built the company up from 1935.

Experiments with fibreglass first appeared in 1954 when the Regal Mk II received a fibreglass hard top and bonnet. *Stuart Cyphus*

At the same time as the 5cwt van Reliant also introduced a 'Utility and 5cwt van' model. This essentially followed the lines of the standard van though was an estate/station wagon model with a fibreglass top that featured large glass windows along each side. Whilst the bonnet was also made of fibreglass, this differed from the van model in that an air scoop had been grafted into the bonnet on the right-hand side. Inside the Utility, extra seating was added with not only a front passenger seat but also a rear bench seat. The seats, side windows and a host of other features like bumpers (that, due to their weight, were optional extras on the standard van) meant that despite its fibreglass implants, the Utility weighed in at 1,008lb making it too heavy to fall into the tricycle class and thus the lower tax that came with that. It was also a lot more expensive, costing £511 7s 0d including Purchase Tax. As a result few Utility vans were sold in the UK with it becoming more of an export model.

Reliant soon realised that, providing the glass matting was not too thick, the fibreglass panels were not just as strong as aluminium but also significantly lighter and so great weight savings could be had. To prove its strength, Williams would proudly jump with his full weight onto a fibreglass transmission tunnel that he kept for the benefit of important visitors. Following further experimentation with fibreglass, a Regal Mk II saloon was announced in November 1955; this now had a fibreglass bonnet and a new, somewhat bulbous looking, fibreglass hardtop. Both were an instant hit and as a result of their success Reliant set about designing a replacement to the Regal Mk II that would have a complete fibreglass body.

Above: The advent of fibreglass also brought along a new commercial model. The Utility and 5cwt van was effectively Reliant's first estate car though it was too heavy to be classed as a tricycle.

Right: Tom Scott hands over paperwork for a left-hand drive Utility and 5cwt van that are bound for Cairo in Egypt.

Based around a Regal Mk II, the 5cwt van set the standard loading capacity for all Reliant vans that were to follow.

North side expansion

As production continued to increase, the issue of space haunted Reliant yet again and the company realised that to succeed making fibreglass parts in large volumes required additional buildings. Whilst it had been expanding on the south side of Watling Street, on the north side, directly opposite it, there was a row of terrace houses and a large plot of unused land that was sandwiched in between two roads, Mount Pleasant on the west side and Parkfield Crescent on the east side. Reliant purchased the land (which was owned by Tolson's estate) in the mid-1950s and set about erecting new buildings that would house the making of fibreglass bodies.

Regal Mk III

In October 1956, Reliant was able to lay claim to the title of producing Europe's first mass-produced full-fibreglass-bodied car with the introduction of the new Regal Mk III. Compared with the box shaped Regal Mk II, the Mk III did not have a straight edge anywhere, instead it had a curvaceous body that also incorporated the dummy wings at the front of the vehicle to resemble those found on a contemporary four-wheeler that gave the Regal a more car-like appearance. The curved body was not just purely for show, however, as detailed earlier, fibreglass is at its strongest when formed into curves rather than laid flat. For additional support, inside the body an ash frame and wooden floor remained, offering rigidity and a means for fastening the body to the chassis. The new body made the Regal Mk III five inches longer and six inches wider, although the rear track remained unaltered. Williams was questioned by the motoring press on how this larger body would affect handling. Williams was completely unconcerned with such doubts and dismissed any notion that three wheelers were less stable than four.

The new body also brought with it flashing indicators (replacing the semaphores on the Mk II) and sliding Perspex windows in the doors. Under the body, the chassis, suspension and steering also remained virtually the same, though the unaltered 747cc side-valve engine was now paired with a synchromesh gearbox. Priced at £430 13s 6d including Purchase Tax the Regal Mk III was sold in both drop-head coupé and hard-top saloon versions and brought with it many admirers. Compared with other three-wheelers on the market, the Regal was still not the cheapest, though it was certainly one of the best looking and continued to remain one of the most practical ones.

The Regal Mk III was Reliant's first all-fibreglass vehicle, with the body reinforced by a wooden frame. It is seen here with Reliant employee Marlene Gaskin. *Marlene Gaskin*

Switching across to the commercial range, both the Utility and the Regal Mk II 5cwt van continued in production until May 1958, when the Utility model was phased out and the van was replaced by the Regal Mk IV 5cwt van several months ahead of the Regal Mk IV saloon. This meant that, although there was not a Regal Mk III based van, as both the Regal Mk IV van and Regal Mk III saloon were being built side-by-side, some vans did contain certain Mk III styling details.

Left: The Regal Mk III demonstrated that the main advantages of fibreglass were not only strength and weight-savings but also the ability to create a body with numerous curves. *Sverker P Zethelius*

Below: Based on the Regal Mk IV, the 5cwt Truck was an attempt by Reliant to reintroduce a pick-up type vehicle. However, sales were disappointing and so the model was phased out. *Thomas Touw*

The first all-fibreglass van came in the form of a Regal Mk IV-based 5cwt van with double doors at the back.

Although almost identical to the Mk III, the Regal Mk IV did have a number of differences, the most obvious being the separate side lights and indicators in addition to the drop-down windows.

ALL
FIBRE-GLASS
BODY

4 CYLINDER
WATER-COOLED
ENGINE

4 SPEED & REVERSE
SYNCHROMESH
GEARBOX

YUE 461

THE
Reliant REGAL Mk.IV

Never before in the history of motoring has a three-wheeler offered so much. The "Regal" Mk. IV has so many outstanding features that the demand increases daily. ★ Non-rusting fibreglass body ★ Four-cylinder water-cooled engine ★ Four-speed and reverse synchromesh gearbox ★ Full four-seater ★ Cruising speed 50 m.p.h. Max. speed 65 ★ Tax £5 per year ★ Low insurance.
No wonder the Reliant "Regal" Mk. IV is "Britain's Finest Three-Wheeler."
Write today for your copy of our latest brochure.

RELIANT ENGINEERING CO (TAMWORTH) LTD
WATLING STREET · TWO GATES · TAMWORTH · STAFFS Phone: Tamworth 336 · Grams: Reliant 336
London Distributor : Glanfield Lawrence (Highbury) Ltd · Reliant House · 28/32 Highbury Corner · N.5

Regal Mk IV

Catching up with the van, the Regal Mk IV saloon arrived in September 1958 and again was an updated version available in saloon and coupé variants. Whilst some improvements were visible, such as the sliding door windows being replaced by drop glass, many of the changes happened under the body; these included the original front torsion bar suspension system and overly complicated double-cranked steering arrangement being replaced. The new system consisted of a simplified suspension system using a box section radius arm with Armstrong combined coil-spring and hydraulic damper and much-simplified steering. This had a drop arm from the steering box with a single track rod to the stub axle; this was to set the trend and was used on all future Reliant three-wheelers. Along with larger section tyres and regrouped foot controls, starting and night time visibility was also improved with the introduction of a 12 volt electrical system (compared with 6 volts in previous Regals).

A Reliant employee, Winifred Mortimer (née Perkins), happily poses with a Regal Mk IV in 1956 for a magazine article. *Winifred Mortimer*

One of the major changes with the Regal Mk IV was the introduction of leading arm suspension on the front wheel; this was controlled by a heavy duty combined coil spring and hydraulic suspension unit.

As a result of its short production run, only a handful of Regal Mk IV cars survive; this example, first registered in 1958, is one of them.

Every young lad's dream: a Reliant Regal Mk V.

Regal Mk V

Production of the Regal Mk IV had barely reached full throttle when, in June 1959, it was replaced by the Regal Mk V, though the Mk IV van was not replaced by the Mk V van until August of that year. Whilst mechanically, the Regal Mk V was virtually identical to the Mk IV, the biggest difference was the body as that had been completely revised. The new shape was a modern design (for the late 1950s) and was both longer and wider than its predecessor. Such was the design of the body, it was only available as a hard-top version with the coupé version now discontinued and assigned to the history books. In addition, it also featured external boot access with a real car-type boot at the rear, separate front and rear bumpers and twin windscreen wipers. The front and rear windscreens were also now formed of safety glass but the door windows reverted to the Perspex sliding glass windows first used in the Regal Mk III.

Left: Along with the Regal Mk V saloon, the 5cwt van was also updated to Mk V specifications.

Below: Taken at Frank Baylis, butchers of Dosthill near Tamworth, Reliant used this photograph for both the Mk V van and Mk VI van brochures as, whilst the models had differences at the front, from the back they were identical.

The Arrival of Ray Wiggin

Towards the late 1950s, Williams was becoming very conscious of his advancing years as his 70th birthday waited just around the corner. Following an illness, Williams had now moved out of the self-contained apartment at Reliant to Long View in Hopwas, Tamworth, where he had a housemaid and a gardener. Having no children, he was well aware that he needed to find a successor for the company he had built up from nothing and which, by 1959, had reached a turnover of £600,000 a year. In the same year Williams had become acquainted with fellow Christadelphian, Ray Wiggin, who was the Chief Estimator at the Stampings Alliance factory in Shenstone, near Lichfield. Wiggin was taken on as Williams' personal assistant, though as John Tracey recalls, on the day Wiggin arrived, Williams took him into a production meeting and informed the staff then that this is the man they will now report to even though Wiggin did not officially become the Deputy Managing Director until 1962.

Regal Mk VI

Ever keen to keep the Regal in the news, the range was updated in November 1960, with the announcement of the Regal Mk VI saloon and Mk VI 5cwt van. Although not dramatically different to the Regal Mk V, the Mk VI now had a much deeper windscreen that provided greater all round visibility. In a bid to improve rear passenger space with increased headroom, the roof of the saloon model was redesigned which resulted in a pronounced bulge over the rear window. Whilst the 5cwt van version still retained separate stop/tail and indicator lights at the rear, the saloon version was fitted with a combined lens unit from an Austin Mini, whilst the front running lights and indicators on both versions were combined in a single unit producing a white flashing indicator. The interior also had a slight makeover and featured a new dashboard equipped, with a large speedometer positioned in the centre.

A Regal Mk VI as displayed at the 1960 Motor Cycle Show.

A Regal Mk VI saloon brochure showing a Mk VI outside the Odeon at Sutton Coldfield.

Left: The final inspection of the Regal Mk VI saloon as it comes off the assembly line. What is also clear is the overhang from the rear window and the neat combined lamp cluster.

Below: The author's ex-Regal Mk VI 5cwt van, seen here wearing its TV make-over for a brief appearance in the film *Toast*.

The side-valve Regal bodies consisted of several main parts attached to a hard wood frame. Here a Regal Mk VI front end is taken for assembly. *RSSOC*

A very cramped fibreglass shop on the south side of the A5 in 1961 produces Regal Mk VI roofs.

Britain's first mass-produced all-aluminium engine

Twenty years after Reliant had designed its own version of the Austin 7 side-valve engine, in 1959 work began on producing a new overhead-valve (ohv) engine that was based on a Chinese copy of a cast iron Standard engine. Headed by Ron Heathcote, who had joined Reliant in 1949, the aim was to produce a new engine that was not only lighter than the old side-valve unit but also required less maintenance. Within a few months, the first prototype was completed, though made from cast-iron and steel, it was 50-60lb heavier that the old side-valve unit. Heathcote knew that, whilst the design was right, the weight itself had to be reduced further and concluded that the only material capable of doing this was aluminium. At that point in time only one vehicle on the market used a substantial amount of aluminium in its engine and that was the Rolls Royce with a cast aluminium alloy cylinder head. Whilst the Reliant Regal may share the same RR initials as the Rolls Royce, their final marketing prices are at opposite ends of the spectrum. However, this did not stop Reliant investing heavily and consulting with Birmal (Birmingham Aluminium) to produce a sand-cast alloy cylinder block followed by the rocker cover and sump. Once Reliant then managed to make a die-casting of the cylinder head in aluminium with Birmal's assistance, it now had all the main components necessary to make an all-aluminium engine. Using a Solex carburettor, the new engine weighed in at 138lb, 20lb less than then old side-valve unit. Whilst weighing less, the cylinder capacity was also reduced from 747cc in the side-valve to 598cc. Heathcote had worked out that in an ohv unit, this was enough to propel the Reliant and would actually provide more power. He was right, once tested the new ohv engine provided 24.2bhp compared with 17.5bhp previously.

Reliant made the proud claim that this was Britain's first mass-produced all-aluminium engine and something that had been done by a relatively small company in Tamworth beating the Rootes Group, with their Coventry Climax-derived Hillman Imp, to the title by just a few months. The engine was initially tested by installing it into several 'Q-Car' Regal Mk VIs that were then driven up and down the M1 motorway and for every journey imaginable with employees being told to take the cars out until 100,000 miles had been reached. At the time the M1 was the only motorway in the UK, having opened just a few years earlier in 1959. The 70mph speed limit* had yet to be introduced and Reliant noted that, despite stories of 190mph test on the M1 by sports cars, and cruising at 100mph, the 'Q-Cars' were driven 'at an average speed of considerably more than 60mph' and were seldom passed by other drivers. The engines were then stripped down and examined; following testing, it was determined that with no visible cylinder bore wear, they would be capable of several thousand more miles without major issues.

In 1966 Reliant was one of many companies who opposed the Government's 70mph speed limit proposals. It expressed support for the 'Motorist Action' group set up to fight the 70mph limit and other restrictive laws affecting motorist. Reliant claimed that: 'Cars for export have to be able to cruise at 80 or 100mph and if this speed limit continues, there is a danger that British manufacturers may be lulled into a false sense of security, which could show up in a decline of quality.'

the *New* 600 c.c. o.h.v. engine

Reliant's 598cc overhead valve engine was Britain's first mass-produced all-aluminium engine.

Regal Mk VI-A

Things were about to change completely again for Reliant with the introduction of the Regal 3/25 saloon fitted with the new ohv engine though, at the time, a Regal 3/25 van version was yet to follow. Therefore, acting as a temporary measure, in October 1962 the Reliant Mk VI-A 5cwt van was announced at the Commercial Motor Show. This was essentially the same vehicle as the earlier Regal Mk VI van, though the traditional side-valve engine had now been replaced by the new ohv unit increasing the power from 17.5bhp to 24.2bhp. This made it the only model in Reliant's history that was available new with either a side-valve or an ohv engine. Produced alongside the Regal 3/25 saloon until May 1963, when a commercial version of the 3/25 was available, the Mk VI-A van was then phased out with just 500 vehicles being built. As the last one left the assembly line it marked the end of an era as, in its Mk VI guise, it not only saw the end of the cast-iron side-valve engine that had served the company so well but it also saw the demise of the traditional wooden frame construction process that was used in the very first Reliant. Whilst the new fibreglass body of the Regal 3/25 was a revolutionary step forward, it did bring with it job losses. The new body did not require wooden reinforcement and consequently the wood compound at Reliant closed in 1963, resulting in those who worked there being made redundant. Although unconfirmed, there are also numerous rumours from various sources that, in preparation for the new ohv engine, Reliant dug a large deep trench at the back of the factory and in it disposed of a number of side-valve engines and tooling to make additional space.

With the arrival of 1960 the Reliant Engineering Co (Tamworth) Ltd celebrated its Silver Anniversary and 25 years of dedicated perseverance had paid off for Williams, whose success more than silenced those who believed such a venture would never work. His Reliant three-wheeler had proved the critics wrong and had become one of the biggest success stories of its time, selling vehicles not only to the UK but also around the world.

Adding an extra wheel

n a 1950 Reliant publication, Tom Williams acknowledged that he has been asked many times 'Why don't you make a four-wheeler?' to which he replied:

'Why should we. The three wheeler has decided advantages over the four wheeler, the myth that it easily turns over has been exploded. I could turn a four wheeler over if I wished.'

It seemed, therefore, as though four-wheelers were something the company would never entertain. However, just eight years later, things did change and Reliant created its first four-wheeler, the Regent Four. Reliant had been exporting the Regent 10cwt three-wheeler to Israel for a number of years, initially to a customer called Schneller, who then sold his business to Itzhak Shubinsky. Shubinsky

was a shipper and an import merchant and he continued to build the business, buying Regents from Reliant in a SKD format. Unlike the UK, three-wheelers in Israel did not benefit from cheaper tax brackets and so Shubinsky suggested to Williams that, if Reliant could produce a four-wheeler, it would have a marketing advantage as it was in direct competition with vehicles from larger manufacturers. Despite Williams' initial belief that the company did not need to make four-wheelers, he did recognise Shubinsky's point and, although Reliant had no experience with four-wheelers, he agreed that they should go ahead and make one.

The restyled Carmel looked a lot sleeker and was hoped would appeal to a great audience.

Regent Four/Sussita

Shubinsky set up a new company called Autocars Ltd in Haifa, Israel and asked Reliant to produce a utility four-wheeler that was tough enough to survive the pounding from Israel's bumpy roads, could carry a 10cwt payload at 50mph (80km/h) and could be built with various bodies offering saloon, station wagon (estate), van and pick-up versions. Reliant responded and created a new chassis that, whilst being very similar to the standard three-wheeler with flanged box-section main members and tubular cross-bracing members, used 16-gauge steel making it both stronger and heavier. As for the front of the chassis, *Commercial Motor* magazine in 1958 noted:

> '... a deep box-section cross member at the front gives rigid support for the independent front suspension, which is of the unequal-wishbone type with coil springs and direct-acting telescopic shock absorbers'.

It was very apparent that the Reliant 747cc side-valve engine was not sufficient enough to power this new four-wheeler and so Reliant turned to Ford using the latter's 1,172cc, water-cooled, side-valve engine as fitted to the Ford Popular. Producing 36bhp at 4,400rpm, this then drove the rear axle via a three-speed synchromesh gear box (also from the Ford Popular) and a needle-jointed propeller shaft. The body of the Regent Four was very reminiscent of that fitted to the three wheeled Regal Mk V van and likewise was made of fibreglass bonded to an ash frame, though was much longer at 12ft 2in (compared with 10ft 8in for the Regal Mk V) and had a modified wider front end to house both wheels.

The first batch of 30 Regent four-wheelers were shipped to Autocars Ltd in Israel on 12 April 1958 as Complete Knock Down (CKD) kits along with components for a prototype fibreglass body, so that bodies could be made in Israel using locally manufactured products. Whilst the chassis and initial body moulds were supplied by Reliant, the engines and gearboxes were sent directly from Ford as complete units. The vehicles were then assembled in both Haifa and Tel Aviv.

Although displayed at the Commercial Motor Transport Exhibition at Earl's Court in 1958, along with a four-wheeled chassis and running gear, while *Commercial Motor* stated the car would be marketed in the UK in the future, the Regent Four is believed to have been an export model only. As production of the Regent Four started, the name was changed in Israel to 'Sussita'. In the five years that followed over 6,000 kits were sent from Reliant to Israel. Various modifications, including changes to the body styling, were made along the way with the most notable being a change in engine in 1962 with the 997cc Ford Anglia 105E now being fitted and offering an extra 3bhp. The Sussita was also briefly sold in the USA and Canada as the Sabra

Whilst the original Sussita resembled the Regent Four, the front was redesigned in this 1963 model.

One of very few UK-registered Sussitas; these were sign written and used by Reliant. *RSSOC*

Resembling a Regal Mk V van, the Regent Four was Reliant's first four-wheel vehicle.

(meaning not only a native of Israel but is also the name of a genus of cactus) and, despite a positive reception at the 1960 New York Trade Fair, it is believed that less than 150 vehicles were actually exported. In addition to the USA and Canada, Autocars was also re-exporting vehicles to countries like Greece, Somalia and Ethiopia.

Carmel

Just after the Sussita went into production and given the success it was finding, Shubinsky believed that the people of Israel also needed a modern family car. This, he planned, would be a car actually designed for that purpose and not a modified Sussita. Shubinsky again contacted Reliant. Within just four months a new two-door family car had been designed and engineered. The new vehicle was to be called the Carmel (named after a mountain that overlooks Haifa) and, like the Regent Four, shared a similar styling to Reliant's three-wheeler range, which at the time was the Regal 3/25. The Carmel had a two-door fibreglass body that, like the Regal 3/25, incorporated a Ford Anglia style reverse slant window. Fitted with a 1,198cc engine from a Ford Anglia Super that produced 47bhp, the car also featured a suspension system that could deal with some of the rough roads in Israel with independent suspension all round, with swing axles at the rear and combined coil springs and dampers at the front.

The reverse angled rear screen looked somewhat at odds with the front angle rear side-light and was a design feature soon modified on the Carmel.

Reliant first created a scale model of the Carmel and shipped it over to Shubinsky; this then soon resulted in an order for 1,500 Carmels. Once production started, it was soon realised that the reverse slant rear window was not that well received and, so within a year, the moulds were changed to create a more traditional style for the rear window. The Carmel, however, was not selling as well as it was hoped with the Sussita still being the vehicle bringing in the sales and so, back at Reliant, David Ogle Associates were employed to redesign both the Carmel and the Sussita; this resulted in the Carmel 12 and the Sussita 12 in 1964. The latter had now pretty much taken on the identity of the Carmel, becoming an estate/station wagon version of it.

Sabra Sport

As detailed previously, in the USA and Canada the Sussita was marketed as the Sabra. Alongside it a much sportier looking version called the Sabra Sport was also offered. Whilst Shubinsky was at the 1960 Sports and Racing Car Show in London, he came across the 1172 body shell, an open sports car body that was being exhibited by a company called Ashley Laminates. At the same show he also saw a new ladder-type chassis that had independent front suspension made by Leslie Bellamy that looked the right size for Ashley's body shell. Autocars bought the design rights to both Ashley's 1172 body shell and Bellamy's chassis and then contacted Reliant asking the company to put both parts together and build a prototype. What Shubinsky thought would be a straightforward task actually became a challenge for Reliant's engineers. Led by

Sabra Sport prototype that used a modified Ashley 1172 body. *Pat Afford*

The Leslie Bellamy chassis used in the Sabra Sport prototype.
Pat Afford

A 1961 Autocars' brochure for the Sabra Sport; note that the over riders are colour coded rather than a chrome finish used on later versions.

from the Meadows Frisky three-wheeler. With a floorpan made of marine-grade plywood, the whole front end of the body tilted forward to expose the engine and front suspension. One final touch asked for by Shubinsky was that, for the American market, large front chrome over-riders should be added.

Once completed, the Sabra Sports prototype made its first appearance at the New York World's Fair in May 1961 and created a lot of interest despite not having a wiring harness or propeller shaft. The plan was that Reliant would supply Autocars with the kits for the Sabra Sports so that the latter could then assemble it and export it to the USA. As Autocars was still busy preparing its workshops, Reliant built the first 100 Sabra Sports cars and shipped them to the USA on Autocars' behalf. In 1962, the Sabra Sports was slightly modified with a revised front end and doors, and a Sabra GT (Gran Tourismo) was added to the range; this was fitted with had a fixed hard top. The hard top later became an option, with ST denoting soft top and HT hard top. All models remained in production until 1965 and, although the Sussita and Carmel continued, Autocars' actual ties with Reliant were severed in the same year when Shubinsky signed a deal with British Leyland. In 1971 Autocars went into liquidation.

Sabre

Reliant saw an opportunity to market the Sabra in the UK and so converted two left-hand drive Sabra sports cars into right-hand drives and changed the spelling of 'Sabra' to 'Sabre' to make them sound more British. The Sabre was exhibited at the 1961 Motor Show at Earl's Court, London and marked Reliant's entry into the sports car market. Opinions about the car, however, were divided, as both the public and dealers alike were unsure of the Sabre's independent front suspension and the large boomerang style chrome over-riders attached to the front, that were originally designed for the American market.

The Sabre (code named SE1 and later known as Sabre Four) was powered by a 1,703cc Ford Consul 375 engine, that was available at an extra cost with stage one and stage two tuning modifications, both of which were undertaken by tuners Alexander Engineering Co of Haddenham. The first stage only offered a minor boost to the overall performance with a single-choke Zenith downdraft carburettor. At an extra cost of £52 10s, the second stage of tuning included twin SU carburettors that gave the Sabre more power, pushing it beyond the 100mph (161km/h) mark on the speedometer. At a price of £1,164 19s 9d, the Sabre was more expensive than a number of its rivals though, whilst it received criticism that the ride was too harsh, it was soon realised that the independent front suspension system actually worked very well on the road. Even more so as it was complemented with rear Girling combined coil springs and shock absorbers, along

Colin Fine-Thompson (E S Thompson's son), the team faced a number of difficulties making various components fit inside the new fibreglass body shell. When fitting the engine, the 1,703cc engine from a Ford Consul was used, primarily because it fitted under the bonnet. Producing 72bhp, the engine was in turn mated to a German ZF four-speed synchromesh gearbox, whilst many other components came from a variety of cars including the Austin Cambridge and Standard Vanguard. Even three-wheeler parts made it into the vehicle with Regal Mk VI coil springs and a windscreen

Above: Exhibited at the 1961 London Motor Show, the Sabre was an Anglicised version of the Sabra restyled for the UK market.

Right: One of the most distinguishing visual points on the Sabre was the large chrome over riders; this produced a very mixed reaction from the general public. *Thomas Touw*

with a modified live rear axle located by a Watts linkage. In a bid to showcase its new sports car, Reliant entered the Sabre into a number of rallies, in which it met with some success.

Sabre Six (SE2)

In October 1961, a new — more powerful — version of the Sabre (the Sabre Six) was displayed at the London Motorshow. Taking on board the general opinions of the front end, the bodywork had been redesigned to incorporate a shorter nosed bonnet, along with rounded rear wheel arches. A number of changes were also made under the bonnet; this saw the inclusion of a more powerful 2,553cc Ford straight six engine that was now mated to a four-speed synchromesh Ford gearbox. Whist early versions kept the same suspension, Reliant then switched to a double wishbone and coil system (which was also the standard setup used on the Triumph TR4) that was supplied direct from Alford & Alder.

The Sabre Six went on sale in 1962 and, with a top speed of 110mph (177km/h), it proved to be a formidable opponent, with Reliant entering a Sabre Six works car into a number of rallies. In 1964, a spectacular crash at the Monte Carlo Rally showed just how strong the Sabre Six was and indeed how strong a glass fibre body is. During the rally, G H F 'Bobby' Parkes and Arthur Senior (who was driving) suffered a burst tyre, which caused the car to swerve off the road. Unfortunately, at that point of the road, there was no retaining wall and the Sabre Six drove over the edge and rolled 80ft down a scree slope, landing nose first onto a road they had just driven up. Amazingly, both Parkes and Senior climbed out of the wreckage with just a few cuts and bruises and hoped to continue driving the car to the finish line. However, despite protecting its crew, the Sabre Six was beyond repair. Perhaps of greater testimony to the car was that the only modifications made to the vehicle for rallying were extra headlamps, with the body being a standard one fitted to all production cars. Despite gaining some success in rallies, the Sabre Six was not a great seller with only 75 Sabre GTs and two Sabre convertibles being made. Compared with larger manufacturers, Reliant was at the time only a fairly small engineering company and, as such, did not have the same level of investment to make on development and eventually the works car was sold off, with the Sabre range coming to an end in 1964.

Legendary comedian and actor, (Sir) Norman Wisdom looks rather delighted with his newly acquired Sabre Six in 1963. The Sabre and the Scimitar that followed were firm favourites amongst many celebrities. *RSSOC*

Above: Reliant entered a number of works cars into various rallies, meeting with some success. The Sabre Six in particular, with a top speed of 110mph (177km/h), proved quite a contender. *Thomas Touw*

Right: During the 1964 Monte Carlo rally, a Sabre Six overshot a hairpin and dropped 70ft down a mountainside onto the road it had just driven up. Such was the strength of the chassis — which was unmodified from production vehicles — both occupants walked away from the crash with just superficial wounds. *RSSOC*

Gwent & West of England Enterprises Ltd

Reliant's financial security was to take a turn for the better in 1962, when Reliant entered into negotiations with Gwent & West of England Enterprises Ltd, spearheaded by Julian Hodge. Having already invested in various sectors, including credit finance, merchant banking, engineering and motor vehicle distribution, Hodge was keen to expand the automotive sector within Gwent & West. The negotiations resulted in 76% of Reliant's shares being sold to Gwent & West for £5 cash plus five and five-sevenths Gwent shares for one Reliant share. Although Hodge now had a seat on the board and was able to inject additional funding for future projects, he took a step back from the day-to day running of Reliant, leaving Williams in charge as the Chairman and Managing Director. Furthermore, investment from Hodge also meant that Reliant was now able to offer hire purchase deals on its vehicles through Hodge Finance.

Regal 3/25

Although the Reliant Sabre was now starting to make a name for itself and become a success for Reliant, it was the three-wheelers that really kept the cash flowing into the company. Despite constant improvements and its increasing popularity, the Reliant Regal range was starting to look very dated, both in appearance and in performance, still being powered by a side-valve engine, particularly when compared with two recent arrivals in the four-wheeled market, namely the Ford Anglia 105E and the BMC Mini. Reliant, therefore, needed a whole new generation of three wheelers and thus went back to the drawing board.

Occasionally referred to by Reliant as a Regal Mk VII, though being completely redesigned from the ground up, the Regal 3/25 was launched in October 1962. Costing £449 (including Purchase Tax) initially, the Regal 3/25 was available only in a saloon format, with the old Regal MK VI van in its Mk VI-A guise continuing to service the needs for the commercial sector. Advertised as a car suitable for four

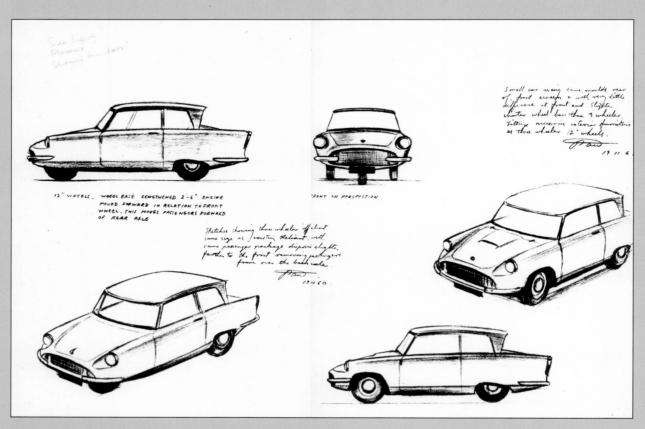

Although the front is much more rounded, these 1960 sketches from Reliant show a clear resemblance to the Regal 3/25 that followed. Interestingly a similar four-wheel version is also shown. *RSSOC*

adults, the Regal 3/25 featured a new fibreglass body that was a unitary construction with both an outer and inner shell (which also included the dashboard moulding) that were bonded together to give it both strength and rigidity, thus removing the need for a wooden frame, as with earlier models. Moving on from the period curves of the side-valve Regals, the 3/25 had a much more car-like appearance that was in keeping with other four-wheel cars of the era, with a large front grille and a backward sloping backlight that was very reminiscent of the Ford Anglia 105E. The whole body unit was simply bolted onto the chassis, which in the Regal 3/25 used much slimmer frame members that were reduced to a depth of 25cm. These also employed lighter leaf springs at the rear that were whittled down from six- to three-leaf design.

One of the biggest changes was the use of the new all-aluminium, water cooled, 598cc, overhead valve engine. Producing 24.5bhp (hence the name of 3/25, being a contraction of three wheels and a rounded-up 25bhp), the 3/25 was a much lighter beast, compared to the Regals of old, and so Reliant could afford the vehicle a few additional luxuries, like wind-up windows with additional opening quarter lights, an ashtray, map pockets in the doors and increased sound proofing around the engine cowling. As an additional creature comfort, one of the extras that was made available for the 3/25 was a Smiths' heating system for £12 that used water from the engine to heat a matrix and then blow the hot air surrounding it into the car.

342 ENX was the first Regal 3/25 off the assembly line and was well-known for its travelling exploits and for proving the reliability of the Regal. Starting from Tamworth, in 1962 it drove 2,500 miles on a proving run through Scandinavia, and then a year later it did the Monte Carlo Rally. Shortly after it then did a 5,211-mile trip to the Sahara desert and back, all without any incidents.

The Regal 3/25 production line in 1962 and what could only be a Regal Mk VI-A van also being assembled.

With its large distinctive front grille, the Regal 3/25 also managed to find a home with the famous. *Photo Storch*

The van version of the 3/25 followed in May 1963 and, as in previous vehicles, had a 5cwt payload. Whilst following the style of the 3/25 saloon, one major change with this van was that it now had a single rear door that opened to the side (compared with twin doors in previous vans). This made it easier to load and helped to reduce the overall weight.

Whilst all Reliant powertrains contained a reverse gear, laws in the UK stated that, if a driver only had a motorcycle licence, the reverse gear had to be blanked off and could not be used. This was applicable to all three-wheelers and not just Reliants, though following discussions between Reliant's Tom Scott and Ernest Marples, the then Minister for Transport, this law was dropped in April 1963 so all drivers, including those with only motorcycle licences, could have a

Unlike previous vans the 5cwt Regal 3/25 based van now featured luxuries, such as a heater and demister, along with a low-level floor for easy loading.

reverse gear. Strangely the misconception that three-wheelers do not have a reverse gear remains. Over 50 years later, much to the author's amusement once whilst driving down a narrow Tamworth street in a 1961 Reliant Regal Mk VI van, I was met by a car coming the opposite way. The street had cars parked on both sides of the road and there was not enough room for either car to pass with the Reliant already having travelled down 85% of the road. The car driver refused to move until the author shouted out of his car window, 'It doesn't have a reverse gear'... the other car reversed back down the street. Naturally the Regal Mk VI does have a perfectly working reverse gear.

Reliant name change

With a desire to further increase its overall self-sufficiency, in September 1963 Reliant formed a new subsidiary called Press Operations Ltd that would manufacture steel chassis members and other pressed steel components for both its own vehicles and other companies. Due to its recent and projected expansion, and as its scope of operations had changed both at home and abroad, a board meeting was held in the same month and it was decided that the parent company of the Reliant Group would change its name from 'Reliant Engineering Co (Tamworth) Ltd' to 'Reliant Motor Co Ltd' with the change officially taking place on 9 October 1963. The new name was

felt to be more fitting, especially as Reliant had moved into both the passenger and sports car markets. Reliant's existing subsidiaries (Morson Engineering Co Ltd, Smiths Forgings Ltd and Press Operations Ltd) all continued with their individual names though the company was now split into two main divisions: a light car division consisting of the manufacture of three-wheelers and a sports car division to manufacture the Sabre range and future sports car projects.

New Shenstone Factory

October 1963 also saw the production of three-wheelers came to a complete stand still for six weeks when on 23 October a fire ripped through the fibreglass shop on the south side of Watling Street, destroying the moulds for all 3/25 and 5cwt van bodies, which were worth at least £10,000. In addition to these, it was estimated that at least £50,000 worth of damage had also been caused as a result of lost stock and building damage. Miraculously, the moulds for the Sabre Six bodies were untouched as they had been moved to a different location just a few weeks earlier.

Reliant had once again found itself short on space and the loss of the fibreglass shop emphasised this even further. To create additional space, Reliant purchased a factory in Shenstone that was just seven miles away from the main site at Two Gates. Built during

World War 2, the building was very familiar to Ray Wiggin, as he had previously worked there when his previous employer, Stampings Alliance, was based there. The new site stood on 13 acres of land, whilst the building had a total floor space of 50,000sq ft. In true Reliant style, to help reduce the cost, the company's own workforce converted the building, resulting in an overall cost of £500,000 for both the building and the refit. Becoming Reliant's new engineering factory, it was officially opened on 27 November 1963 by World Champion racing driver, Jim Clark, who also got to take his first drive in a Regal 3/25. Reliant's new factory meant that it was able to double existing production by manufacturing around 400 engine and gearbox units a week. The factory also manufactured rear axles and suspension units for the company's three-wheel range and, in addition, built all the non-engine mechanicals for the Sabre Six Sports and GT cars. Space was also found at Shenstone for Reliant's subsidiary company Morson Engineering Co Ltd, which was set up in a smaller shop covering an area 5,000sq ft whilst Press Operations Ltd was found a space at the Two Gates site.

Williams was undeniably exceptionally proud of Reliant's new extension with the company's *Reliant Review* newspaper (started just a few months earlier) quoting him as saying:

'When I started the company in 1935, I never realised that Reliant would become Britain's biggest manufacturer of

three-wheeled vehicles. When I look at Shenstone I realise just how far the company has come since I built the prototype Reliant in a garden shed.'

Right: A rare shot of the fire in 1963 that took hold of the buildings on the south side. *John Tracey*

Below: The new engineering plant at Shenstone.

By December 1963, work had already begun on a new glass fibre shop on the north side of Watling Street though limited production of the Regal 3/25 had been resumed by temporarily moving the production of bodies to the old machine shop that was now vacant, following the transfer of engineering operations to Shenstone.

Left: Tom Williams with World Champion racing driver, Jim Clark, at the opening of the new engineering plant at Shenstone. *RSSOC*

Below: Cylinder blocks in production at the Shenstone plant.

Above: A 200-ton press used by Press Operations. This particular machine performed 225,000 separate pressings each week.

Right: Reliant published its own newspaper, the *Reliant Review*, from October 1963 to July 1977; this was seen as a new form of contact between Reliant and owners of its vehicles.

Loss of its founding fathers

After 30 years of loyal service to Reliant, on 21 February 1964, E S (Tommo) Thompson retired on his 65th birthday, though he continued to remain on the company's board of directors. On his final day, Thompson was awarded a gold Omega watch by Williams, along with a cabinet of carpenter's and engineer's tools, the photographs of the occasion were to be the last taken of Williams.

In the same month, Williams resigned as Managing Director, handing over the reins to his successor, Ray Wiggin, though he remained as the chairman. Less than a week later, on 4 March 1964, Williams suffered a heart attack whilst working at his desk and was initially driven home by Wiggin before then being admitted to Burton-on-Trent hospital. Williams died the following day at 5:30pm and, after a private service at his house, the funeral was held on 10 March at the Methodist Church in Aldergate, Tamworth. Due to the number of

Tom Williams and E S Thompson at the latter's retirement presentation. Photographs of this event were the last ones taken of Williams.

E L Rock, the works superintendent, inspects Regal 3/25 5cwt vans on the production line.

people attending, the Christadelphian Church had approached Tamworth Methodists, to ask if they would allow the service to take place there as it was a larger church. The service not only saw his immediate family (including his wife Doris whom he had married just two years earlier) and colleagues from Reliant but was attended by scores of representatives from all of the companies Reliant dealt with,

including Itzhak Shubinsky, the Chairman and Managing Director of the Autocar Co in Israel, who made the 3,000-mile journey by air. Following the funeral the interment then took place at Glascote Cemetery. Prior to his death, Williams had seen Reliant grow from a one man firm to a company employing almost 1,000 people and producing 10,000 vehicles a year, all in just under 30 years. With Wiggin now at the helm there was a sudden burst of activity as Wiggin decided to launch a renewed attack upon the sports car market with the introduction of the much more mass-appealing Scimitar GT. The development of this vehicle developed the relationship between Reliant and the Letchworth-based industrial design company, Ogle Design and its Managing Director, Tom Karen. With such major expansion taking place within the Reliant model range, in April 1965, Gwent & West of England Enterprises Ltd decided to merge the Reliant Motor Co into another of its subsidiaries. This was Hodgkinson Bennis Ltd, which was a Manchester-based engineering company. The merger enabled the Reliant Motor Co to become part of a public limited company, under the Hodgkinson Bennis banner, and thus raise capital for any future projects it might have.

Returning to the Regal 3/25, the vehicle was proving to be a huge success for Reliant and by the end of 1964, 15,000 Regal 3/25 saloons and vans had been manufactured and sold. Things improved further as 1965 arrived, as in the first four months, the Regal 3/25 broke all previous production and sales records. Reliant dealers were jubilant as they reported sales up to three times higher than the average.

Regal 3/25 Super

Until now the Regal had been without competition, as there were no other three-wheelers on the market that offered family motoring in a true car-like vehicle. This was soon to change when, in 1965, Bond Cars Ltd, purchased a Regal 3/25 and, after reverse engineering it to see what made it so successful, decided to produce its own contender to battle the Regal for its crown. News of this hit Reliant and knowing it had to make a counterattack, the company looked at what it could do with the Regal 3/25 so that it would have something new to exhibit when the new Bond model was launched. Ogle Design Ltd was asked to redesign the Regal 3/25, though not with a heavy hand, as there were certain aspects of the 3/25 that Reliant wanted to retain, like extra headroom, knowing these were what made the car successful with customers. The result was a new 3/25 that, whilst essentially being the same vehicle that had been introduced in 1962, had a completely fresh look. Along with a new interior, the front and rear ends had now been restyled with the most dramatic visual change being the replacement of the original large radiator grille with a much smaller split grille. This also allowed the bonnet to be lowered slightly, with the built in bumper extended further down the sides to help reinforce the body. This was then complemented by separate sidelights and indicators (though this changed on later models), whilst at the rear a much more functional boot was incorporated with a lower body line, so that heavy baggage did not need to be lifted so high for loading.

Announced at the Brighton Cycle & Motor Show in September 1965 as the Regal 3/25 Super Saloon and, at the same cost as the old model (£486 14s 2d), the battle with Bond commenced. With the recent news of record sales still in its minds and acknowledging that the previous 3/25 was pretty much a new model, Reliant decided not to withdraw the old model from the market just yet but to offer both variants side-by-side. As a result, the original 3/25, was now renamed as the 3/25 Standard and offered at the reduced price of £468 11s 8d. This act alone caught the attention of the press and gave Reliant the publicity it desired with news of a car manufacturer that actually reduced its pricing of old models to introduce a new one at the same price. The styling of the 3/25 based van remained unchanged with a price tag of £386 10s 0d.

On show was also the Bond 875 which also gained a lot of interest, especially being powered with an 875cc Hillman Imp engine, designed and developed by Coventry Climax that was said to propel it at speeds of over 100mph (161km/h). The vehicle on show was a prototype and was actually overweight and so technically didn't qualify for the three-wheeler tax bracket. As a result, production was delayed as the excess weight was carved off and the engine detuned as it had been found to be too powerful, causing stability issues. By the time it went into production it was quite a different machine, though many of the original order-placers had waited so long they cancelled and bought a Regal. As it turned out, Reliant need not

Top: With a more refined nose, the Regal 3/25 Super looked a much sleeker vehicle. Meanwhile two gents at the back use one of the oldest tricks in the book, holding up a white sheet to ease blanking out the background once the photo is processed.

Middle: With a claimed fuel consumption of 65mpg (4.3 litre/100km), Reliant envisaged that visiting a garage for petrol would be something of a rarity for the Regal 3/25 Super owner. *Thomas Touw*

Bottom: Reliant tested each vehicle for leaks with a waterproof test; here a Regal 3/25 Super is driven through a wash where numerous water jets spray the car from various angles.

Above: Along with a new body and engine, the Regal 3/25 also had a new chassis with the rear of the chassis no longer angled down behind the wheels.

Left: The 5cwt Supervan was based on the Regal 3/25 Super with a revised front end. This was followed by the Supervan II in 1967 (which featured increased bhp due to engine modifications) and the Supervan III in 1968, which was based on the 3/30 version with a 700cc engine.

Bond's contender to the Regal came in the form of the Bond 875 fitted with an 875cc Hillman Imp engine. *Thomas Touw*

have been concerned about keeping the original 3/25 (Standard) saloon in production or the Bond 875 damaging sales, as demand for the Regal 3/25 Super Saloon set a new all-time production record in December 1965, with 100 examples rolling off the production line in a single working day.

New Kettlebrook plant

Following the fire in the glass-fibre shop in October 1963, a new fibreglass shop was built on the north side of Watling Street. Production was again in full swing when, in March 1966, history repeated itself when another fire again destroyed the fibreglass shop. This time it also spread across to the paint shop causing £150,000 worth of damage in addition to destroying two vehicles, valuable spraying equipment and paint supplies.

What followed was perhaps one of the greatest acts of solidarity and loyalty that any company could wish to have. Within a few hours of the fire being extinguished, Wiggin had finalised the purchase of a new site that formerly belonged to Thompson & Southwick Ltd, an iron and brass foundry that had been there since 1863. Situated at the bottom of Basin Lane in Kettlebrook, Tamworth opposite the Coventry

In 1966 a second fire tore through the fibreglass shop. A neighbour, Pamela Wilson, recalls as a child being woken up in the middle of the night to a series of bangs as the flames rapidly spread across the length of the building.

The Kettlebrook site as it stood in 1963 shortly after it was purchased by Reliant.

Canal, the site consisted of six acres of land whilst the building offered 70,000sq ft of floor space. Needing to be completely refitted and, following full union support, production workers were given picks and shovels and sent to the site to begin converting the ex-foundry. Furthermore, whilst production workers were paid anywhere from half to two-thirds of their standard salaries, the company also paid around 300 workers £16 a week to stay at home. Many of those who could have stayed at home decided to switch to emergency work and arrived onsite to help get the Kettlebrook site up and running as quickly as they could. Working in shifts that operated round the clock, what on paper should have took several months to complete, took just four weeks, with the new factory not only up and running but running at full capacity by April 1966. In that time, Reliant lost a further £750,000 in turnover and paid an additional £100,000 by continuing to pay its workers. Employing approximately 600 people at the Kettlebrook site and able to produce 35 bodies per eight-hour shift, Reliant became the largest user of fibreglass in Europe.

Supervan

Partly due to the fire destroying the fibreglass shop and partly in light of the sales boom for the Regal 3/25 Super, the Regal 3/25 Standard saloon was finally discontinued during March 1966. The Regal 3/25 van remained in production until May 1966 when that was replaced by the Super Saloon-based 5cwt Supervan. With a price tag of £396 10s 0d, the Supervan, like the Standard version, featured a single, side-hinged, rear door that had now been strengthened and again featured rear passenger seats as an optional extra.

7 and 10cwt pick-up

It wasn't just in the UK that sales were booming for Reliant. Under the directorship of Wiggin, the company had also embarked on a worldwide sales drive in which the Regal and Supervan found many buyers. Despite this success, Wiggin realised that the three-wheeler range needed a new model that was able to exploit the 'harsher' regions of the world. This was answered in the form of a new 7cwt (355.6kg) capacity 3/25 pick-up model that was announced during May 1966. The 7cwt pick-up was identical mechanically to the UK market models and was powered by the same 598cc engine. It was essentially a Supervan with the rear part of the bodywork removed, leaving a bare chassis. The chassis itself was elongated via a 14in extension that was added into the chassis making the overall length 3,581mm. Fitted with a longer Hardy Spicer or BRD needle-bearing propeller shaft, variable mounting points were also attached to the chassis that allowed any special-application rear bodywork to be fitted, although Reliant did offer a standard wooden pick-up body.

Below left: Due to Greek government regulations relating to vehicles of this class, all Regal 10cwt pick-ups were painted dark green.

Below: Part of the author's collection, this is a four-page mock-up of a 7cwt pick-up brochure created by Reliant. However, the model was soon changed to a 10cwt and so (to date) it is believed this brochure remained a one off.

RELIANT REGAL 7 CWT PICK-UP

Economical   Reliable   Versatile

One of a batch of 100 Regal 10cwt pick-ups being loaded aboard the *Tanta* (3,000 tons) at Liverpool on its way to Greece.

Shortly after the 7cwt had been launched it was discovered that the pick-up could easily manage a 10cwt (507.9kg) payload. To help accommodate this, the chassis was stretched slightly further to an overall length of 3,651mm and the ground clearance was also raised from 6in (152mm) to 8.5in (216mm) with higher suspension. The 10cwt pick-up vehicle rapidly found favour in Canada, France and Greece amongst other places, although it was never to be offered on the home market. The 10cwt pick-up was built for just over a year with around 3,000 vehicles being made when it was then replaced by the TW9.

Regal 3/25 Super Deluxe/ Supervan II

In the UK, hire purchase deposit rates for three-wheelers and motorcycles were slashed from 40% to 25% during 1967, leading to yet another boom in Reliant three-wheeler sales. In September 1967, Reliant unveiled a new engine. The Reliant 598cc all-alloy engine had quickly built itself a reputation as a flexible and reliable power source, not just for the Regal 3/25 but for its ever-growing desirability as a replacement at the lighter end of amateur motorsport. Reliant, of course, kept an interested eye on the 750 racers and their sometimes impressive modifications to the 598cc engine. This, no doubt, influenced the new version unveiled for September 1967 in which changes to the cylinder head, exhaust manifold and a new carburettor increased available engine power from 24.5 to 26bhp at 5,250rpm. The introduction of this new improved engine coincided with the replacement of the Regal 3/25 Super Saloon and 5cwt Supervan by the Regal 3/25 De Luxe saloon and 5cwt Supervan II respectively. At the same time, a third new Regal was added to the range in the form of the Regal 21E. This was introduced as a limited-production 'luxury' model and was priced at £583 2s 4d, almost £65 more than the 3/25 De Luxe. The 21E was so called as it was fitted with 21 extras as standard equipment over the basic De Luxe model. These

Sales Director Tom Scott, George Jenkins (Senior Assembly Shops Foreman), Ray Wiggin and part of the Reliant workforce celebrate as the 50,000th Regal 3/25 leaves the assembly line in June 1968.

This Regal 3/25 21E actually appears as a Regal 3/30 21E in Reliant brochures with the separate side-lights cleverly painted out to give the impression of a later model.

were: additional colours complete with coach line, carpet covered heelboards, carpeted footwell surrounds, interior paintwork matching exterior, chrome-plated speedometer bezel, ammeter and oil gauges with chrome plated surround, chrome plated bonnet hinges and boot hinges and 21E badge, padded sun visors, chromed over-riders front and rear, Lucas spot light and fog light, chromed hub caps and full circle wheel trims, locking petrol filler cap, chrome wing mirrors, spare wheel and a cover, leather effect steering wheel glove, and chrome filler strip in window surrounds.

The author's ex-1972 Supervan III 5cwt van (*Ole Blue*) seen here during a photoshoot for a classic car magazine.

Regal 3/30/Supervan III

It was all change again for the Regal 3/25 when, in August 1968, it was fitted with the new 701cc engine from the Reliant Rebel resulting in the Regal 3/25 De Luxe, 21E and Supervan II becoming the Regal 3/30, 21E-700 and Supervan III respectively. (The 3/30 now signifying the engine had 29.5bhp that was rounded off to 30.) With the exception of a new top speed of 70mph (113km/h) and optional lower ratio in the Supervan III's rear axle (now 4.375:1 instead of 5.14:1), the Regal 3/30 range was otherwise the same as before.

Reliant was now expanding at such a rate that by December 1968 it was a more profitable concern than the officially larger Hodgkinson Bennis Co with which it had been merged back in 1965. Reliant was now responsible for 83% of overall turnover in the business compared with Hodgkinson Bennis's 17%. As a result a decision was taken by the shareholders of Hodgkinson Bennis to allow the Reliant Motor Co to become the dominant element in the business with effect from 31 December 1968 with the thus-newly-formed Reliant Motor Group Ltd replacing the Hodgkinson Bennis name on the London Stock Exchange Register. In the same year British Motor

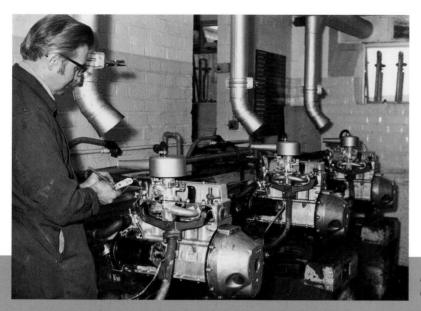

Holdings and Leyland Motors merged to form British Leyland Motor Corporation, which now resulted in Reliant being the largest independent motor manufacturer in the UK and the second largest British-owned motor company. Only the newly formed British Leyland produced more vehicles than Reliant. The gap, however, was quite large with Reliant producing around 20,000 vehicles a year, compared with British Leyland producing just over one million.

Following changes in the 1967, budget the Purchase Tax on the Supervan had been dropped boosting the proposition of owning a three-wheel van. Quick to respond, Reliant increased the manufacture of Supervans from around 5,000 vehicles in

Left: Peter Saunders, chief engine tester, gives the 100,000th OHV engine an *OK* label and the final stamp of approval as it passes a hot run in April 1972.

Due to its popularity the Regal appeared everywhere. Here actor Patrick Cargill awards a lucky winner (George Carter) the show's gold prize of a Regal 3/30 saloon in the TV series *The Golden Shot* in 1970. *Kerry Croxton*

1968 to almost 9,000 vans in 1969. To further increase its desirability, in April 1969 a 21E version of the Supervan III was added to the range. Costing £496, this essentially had the same extras as the saloon version with the exception of the chrome over-riders at the rear of the vehicle as, if fitted, they obstructed the rear door, restricting its opening. To make up the 21 extras, therefore, the Supervan III version featured an interior at the back of the van being painted. By 1970, Supervan sales were surpassing those of the saloons, as not only companies were buying them, but private individuals were also taking advantage of the lower purchase price. In the same year, all models received an interior makeover with three different interior trim colours that were said to give it a Scimitar GTE look, though didn't quite actually achieve this. A year later a range of new colours was introduced, helping to boost sales further. Production of the Regal showed no signs of slowing down and, in December 1972, the 100,000th Regal, an April yellow saloon, left the production line amongst a cheer from the workers. When Roger Musgrave, Reliant's Marketing Manager, was interviewed by the local news programme *ATV Today* about it, the reporter quipped, 'In actual fact though it looks exactly the same as all the others' to which Musgrave replied with a smile, 'Well of course it is, it's bound to be isn't it'. A year later, an interior trim colour change was introduced when the tan-coloured interior replaced the previous black one. Although sales were still climbing, Reliant had been contemplating a Regal replacement, the TW8, since the mid-1960s, although nothing of note was undertaken before the end of 1971, such was the success of its predecessor; however, in October 1973 the Regal finally came to an end. The Regal was not only Reliant's bestselling three-wheeler but also the most successful three-wheeler in the world with over 110,000 of the model being built. Waiting in its nest to replace them was perhaps Reliant's most famous three-wheeler ever — the Robin.

Top: On 6 December 1972, the 100,000th Regal left the production line. The car was kept by Reliant and lent to dealers so they could put it on display for various promotions.

Middle : The 5cwt Supervan III (based on the Regal 3/30) was a firm favourite with many companies both large and small. This particular vehicle was one of 16 that were employed by the East Midlands Electricity Board.

Bottom: Karen Langstaff, Dairy Queen of 1972, with a cut-away Regal 3/30. Reliant was a great fan of producing display models like this to show both how strong and how compact the vehicle was.

Bearing chassis number 003 and displayed by Reliant at the 1964 Earl's Court Motor Show, this particular vehicle is classed as the first true Scimitar GT built, with chassis 001 never been used on a finished car and 002 being registered as an Ogle Scimitar. *Dave Poole*

Scimitar GT

Jumping over to the sports car range, the Sabre Six was starting to look a bit dated and, whilst Ray Wiggin was at the 1962 Motor Show in London, he came across a car that caught his eye. It was designed by David Ogle (of David Ogle Ltd, later known as Ogle Design Ltd) and was based on the Daimler Dart SP250 chassis and used a 2.5-litre V8 engine. Initially, it had been commissioned by Boris Forter, the Managing Director of the Helena Rubenstein (UK) company; however, in May 1962, halfway through its development, David Ogle

was killed in a car crash. The design was completed by Tom Karen, who also had to also create the interior and get the prototype car ready for Earl's Court in October of the same year where it was exhibited as the Ogle SX250. Another SX250 was built for Forter after he gave the prototype to his girlfriend but further cars that he hoped his friends would order were never made.

Reliant had already approached Ogle Design and asked to buy the rights for it and, whilst Daimler initially showed some interest in it, the latter did not use the design and so, following further dialogue, the start of what would be a long relationship between Ogle Design

As soon as it was launched in 1964, the Scimitar GT was immediately acclaimed for its elegant looks and power with a top speed approaching 120mph (193km/h).

and Reliant was formed with the first plan to work together adapting the Sabre Six platform. Reliant set about building a prototype on a Sabre Six chassis that was modified by David Page, with an elongated wheelbase. Reliant's body construction differed substantially from David Ogle's and so the whole body had to be remodelled, but just enough so that it remained a sports car whilst also a four-seater suitable for two adults up front and two children in the back. Under the bonnet it retained the same straight six engine from the Sabre Six; this now included triple SU carburettors as standard and produced 120bhp that provided a top speed of 117mph (188km/h). Following on from the name Sabre, the new car was called the Scimitar GT (SE4) and made its first public appearance at the 1964 Earl's Court Motor Show alongside Reliant's other new four-wheeler, the Rebel. Priced at £1,292 1s 3d, the Scimitar drew much admiration from both the public and the press, with the latter praising it for its sleek design and performance figures with a 0-60mph (0–96km/h)

Ray Wiggin is remembered by his daughter Ruth as being a very hands-on MD who would collect a car at random from the production line on a Friday evening, drive it home and spend time driving it 'hard' whilst talking into his dictaphone giving his report on any noises he heard or on the ride-quality. *RSSOC*

The Scimitar GT assembly line; also note cars on the left being covered in aprons to protect the polychromatic paintwork finish as mechanicals are fitted.

Below: Covered in 43sq ft of Sundym safety glass, the Triplex Ogle GTS was a one-off Scimitar that was also used by the Duke of Edinburgh as a personal vehicle for a while. *Thomas Touw*

of just 10 seconds, a figure that was on par with that of the Lotus Cortina — one of its main competitors. Whilst wire spoke wheels and comprehensive instrumentation came as standard, a number of optional extras were also available; these included a radio, front seat belts, electric sun roof, a ZF type gearbox, and a choice of the De Normanville model 230 overdrive unit.

Triplex GTS

In 1964, a one-off Scimitar was created in the form of the Triplex Ogle GTS. Triplex Safety Glass Co Ltd, makers of automotive safety glass, commissioned Ogle Design to design and build a show car that would demonstrate new glass technology in the form of laminated Sundym glass. Ogle then used a Scimitar GT body shell and after various modifications produced the GTS (Glazing Test Special) with the distinctive number plate of 660 GLE. (These were illegally respaced as 66 0GLE that initially upset the police.) The GTS was covered in 43squ ft of safety glass with a heat-absorbing glass roof, curved round side windows. The Sundym glass used in the roof and side windows contained a trace element of ferrous oxide which helped to increase the absorption of ultra violet and infra-red rays, which reduced the

transmitted radiant heat into the car's interior (this itself having a matt finish to help reduce glare). Apart from the Sundym glass, the car also featured bonding the glass to the body to replace the usual rubber sections. In addition to the usual heated tailgate glass, the car was fitted with an electrically-heated front windscreen.

The Triplex Ogle GTS was featured at the 1965 London Motor Show and was then driven to the Turin Motor Show by two journalists (Basil Cardew of the *Daily Express* and Tom Wisdom of the *Daily Mirror*), where it was admired by many Italian designers and voted the showpiece of the exhibition. It also became the first Reliant to be used by the Royal Family after catching HRH the Duke of Edinburgh's eye; he then bought the vehicle for his own personal use for two years, after which it was repurchased by Triplex and loaned to the National Motor Museum at Beaulieu. The car was then purchased by Reliant enthusiast and author, Don Pither, and on his death in 2002 was shipped to the USA, where it now belongs to Professor Carl Olson.

The buzz surrounding the GTS was creating much publicity for Reliant and, in 1965, the company made its very first entry, a Scimitar GT, into the Institute of British Carriage & Automobile Manufacturers' Coachwork Competition. The Scimitar GT was entered in class 11 for cars with an enclosed coachwork costing between £1,000 and £1,200

From 1967 the Scimitar GT was available with both a 2.5- and 3-litre engine, although the latter was not as popular as Reliant envisaged.

1968 Scimitar GT SE4b powered by a 3-litre engine. *Dave Poole*

exclusive of Purchase Tax. It then made history by winning a silver medal and becoming the first car with a fibreglass body to win a prize. With a view to continue developing the car, in April 1966 John Crosthwaite was taken on as part of Reliant's design and development team becoming the company's chief engineer. Crosthwaite had much experience with the construction and design of lightweight racing cars in addition to working on Indy Cars in the USA. His expertise was soon to enhance the GT when, in the same year, Ford discontinued the 2.6-litre engine and replaced it with the new 3-litre Essex engine that was used in the latest MK IV Ford Zodiac.

Under Crosthwaite's guidance, Reliant set to work redeveloping the Scimitar GT. This was not only to get the new engine to fit in but also to ensure that the performance and handling were the best he could make it. As the new engine was shorter, it was mounted further back to improve weight distribution. Along with adding an anti-roll bar, the lower wishbones were repositioned, the tower structures and an additional cross member added to the chassis. To help handling further, the wire spoke wheels were replaced with wider steel wheels and a higher ratio rear axle was specified. Along with a mechanical overhaul, the car was also updated cosmetically with a new all-black interior that included black instrument dial bezels. Ventilation was also improved with directional variable ventilator jets, as was safety with a collapsible steering column that used two universal joints. With so many improvements incorporated, the new GT became known as the Scimitar GT SE4a.

The Scimitar GT continued to be improved with a SE4b model in late 1966; its main changes were an interior that now featured a new centre console and switch layout. In the same year, Reliant also started to develop a Scimitar GT automatic; however, this made little progress. Interest in the new Scimitar was such that Reliant's Tom Scott was now negotiating with companies in the USA and Canada that were interested in importing the Scimitar. The 3-litre version was exhibited in 1967 at shows in Geneva, Frankfurt and Amsterdam and found a place on the European market. On the home market the 3-litre version was not quite as well received as Reliant had hoped and so, in 1967, it introduced a less powerful version in the Scimitar GT SE4c. Whilst both vehicles looked the same externally, the only significant difference was the engine size badge on the boot-lid, as the SE4c was fitted with a Ford 2.5 litre V6 Essex engine. The car was still said to hit speeds of over 110mph (177km/h), though it offered slightly better fuel economy and perhaps more importantly, the price was £121 cheaper than the 3-litre version. The Scimitar GT continued to be made until November 1970 when it was then replaced with a car that numerous car manufacturers would attempt to replicate, the Scimitar GTE.

The Rebel claimed the title of being the first model from a new manufacturer to enter the British family car market since before World War 2.

Rebel

Whilst historically, Reliant had always been associated with three-wheelers, the new sports car range had proved that Reliant was not a one-trick pony and could produce a serious sports car that could more than stand up for itself in the market place. Whilst the three-wheelers remained the bread and butter of the company, Wiggin, amongst others, was sceptical as to whether the car would always be so popular and believed that, to stay in business, Reliant needed to break into the small car market. To do this, it was determined that they would need to produce their own small four wheeled family car, to be called the Rebel, that was easy to maintain, robust, durable and capable of at least 60mph (96km/h) and 60mpg (4.7 litre/100km).

Tom Karen of Ogle Design was contacted to create a design for a small, modern four-wheeler that would utilise as many Reliant components as it could that were already used in other models. Reliant also wanted to ensure that, whilst the vehicle would have a fibreglass body, it would be much more robust than that used on its three-wheel Regal counterpart. At the same time, Dave Page, from Reliant's development department, and his team set to work building a new ladder type chassis. The chassis was similar to the Regal three-wheeler; however, it was much stronger, using a conventional four-wheel configuration that utilised a steering box from a Standard Ten with wishbones, trunnions and ball-joints from the Triumph GT6/Vitesse. The first prototype proved to be underpowered and, after further tweaking of the 598cc Reliant engine, the power was increased from 24 to 28bhp; this gave the vehicle enough power to meet its specifications of 60mph (96km/h) and 60mpg (4.7 litre/100km).

The four-wheeled layout meant that the engine could be mounted further forward in the chassis; this instantly endowed the interior of the Rebel with a generous amount of space in the front. Fitted with independent front suspension that included inclined coil springs and unequal wishbones, the turning circle was just 27ft. The Rebel body used certain styling traits from the Scimitar GT, with the design also blending in the doors from the Regal whilst the interior had a more luxurious feel than that of the three-wheel range.

Launched with the Scimitar GT at the September 1964 Earl's Court Motor Show, the new Rebel was advertised with the slogan, 'no need for a garage' (a phrase that was actually registered by Reliant) on account of its rust-proof body. With a tongue-in-cheek publicity campaign that warned British Leyland that it had better watch out, the Rebel was not designed for mass production and realistically was never going to compete with cars of the day like the Austin Mini, Ford Anglia or the Hillman Imp. Indeed, with a £524 15s 5d price tag, the Rebel was more expensive than all of them. Reliant, however, was depending on brand loyalty — hoping that owners of Reliant three-wheeler would progress on to the Rebel; however, it didn't happen and sales of the Rebel remained relatively low.

A year later, at the October 1965 Earl's Court Motor Show, a Mk 2 version of the Rebel was showed. This featured, along with a more refined rear suspension, a revised front end with the dummy slats being filled in, giving the front end a much smoother and more modern appearance. Internally, the dashboard and instruments

Right: Long before the days of *Photoshop*, Reliant was a master at retouching photographs and making older models appear as newer ones. Here a note to the artist asks him to paint out the top dummy grille — or 'grill' (sic) — on this Rebel and then paint in a new emblem.

Below: On the left, the Rebel as it was launched in 1964 and, on the right, the revised version introduced in 1966 with, amongst other features, a restyled grille.

Above: The Rebel assembly line seen here in 1967.

Left: This particular shot of a Rebel 750 estate was aimed at the sportsman who needed an economical vehicle with plenty of luggage space.

were updated and capped off with a two-spoke steering wheel that replaced the three-spoke type from the Regal 3/25. With the new Kettlebrook site opening in 1966, Reliant was able to dedicate more space to the Rebel and increase production, which resulted in the Rebel selling in better numbers; however, these were still fairly low, with 163 sales in 1966 and 334 in 1967.

One of the main criticisms about the Rebel was that it was too slow, especially when compared with other small four-wheelers of the era. It was, therefore, decided that a more powerful engine was

required. Reliant then experimented with a Rebel 1600 GT prototype — code named FW6 — that was fitted with a 1,599cc Ford Crossflow engine that, at the time, was used in the Ford Cortina (Mk 2) 1600E. The prototype was road legal and, when tested, was found to outperform its sportier brother, the Scimitar. Reliant, however, decided not to put it into production and instead set about modifying the 598cc engine and increasing the capacity to 701cc. Whilst the power was only marginally increased to 31bhp, the torque output had been increased from 31.5lb at 3,000rpm to 38 at 2,500rpm. This, along with a new Zenith downdraught carburettor, was enough to now push the top speed of the Rebel up to 70mph (113km/h) whilst still retaining 45-55mpg (6.3-5.1-litre/100km) in everyday use. Now called the Rebel 700, a few other modifications were made; these included a new padded dashboard and steering wheel. The latter also provided a combined multi-function switch for horn, indicators and headlight dipper. Whilst visually, the body remained the same, underneath it the chassis had been modified and now tapered towards the front, and the fuel tank was moved, allowing the floor at the rear to be lowered, increasing load space. The Rebel 700 was exhibited at the October 1967 Motor Show and was joined by a Rebel 700 Estate. The Estate version was nine inches longer than the saloon, measuring 12ft 2in and, as a result, was also £30 more expensive at £599 14s 2d

Introduced in 1969, the Rebel estate (seen here with a FW5 on the right) found a successful market in West Africa.

including tax. Despite being more expensive, by 1969, the Estate version (with 46cu ft of luggage space) was selling better than the saloon with around two Estates selling to every one saloon. The Rebel 700 was now also finding a market abroad, with the first exports being to Angola in Western Africa, closely followed by Bermuda and then Portugal, along with the Caribbean islands.

By 1971, a van version was also added to the range on a trial basis. With a 5cwt capacity, the van was essentially an estate version without the rear fibreglass panels being cut out to fit windows. With no passenger seats the van was available in primer only; however, only 29 vans were sold in the first year. Reliant tweaked its engine again in October 1972 to increase the capacity to 748cc, which, due to the compression ratio of 8.5:1, produced 35bhp in the saloon and estate, and with a ratio of 7.5:1 32bhp in the van. This increased the top speed to around 75-80mph (121-128km/h). Powered by the new engine, the Rebel range was now renamed to become the Rebel 750 saloon, estate and van. The 750 range were fitted with a new 'Scimitar look' black interior with a new range of colours; however, sales continued to decline, with just over 300 vehicles a year being sold. After the introduction of the Robin three-wheeler in 1973, Reliant decided, in May 1974, to pull the plug on the Rebel in order to free up much needed production capacity for the Robin.

Turkey — FW5/Anadol

The success of Autocars in Israel with the Sussita and Carmel had not gone unnoticed and a number of other companies in surrounding countries were looking on, keen to emulate them. In Turkey, renowned businessman, Vehbi Koç, who already owned a Ford franchise, importing Ford motor vehicles into the country, also wanted to build a car indigenous to Turkey. Realising that Reliant was the company behind Autocars, he contacted the company in 1963 and asked it to design and develop a car for the Turkish market. This, incidentally, would be the first passenger car built in Turkey. The Koç organisation wanted a car that was bigger than Autocars' Carmel and was large enough to use as a family car, seating four to five people. In addition, the new vehicle needed to be simple in its design with a body that could easily be adapted to produce a range of body styles. By early 1964, work had begun on the new car, codenamed FW5, with Reliant contracting Tom Karen at Ogle Design to design a two-door saloon car that was comparable in size to a Ford Cortina. Reliant's David Page also set to work the design of the h-frame chassis with independent front suspension. Once completed, the FW5 had a greater ground clearance than normal to tackle tough Turkish roads. Whilst the weight was kept below 18cwt to qualify for lower road tax, the design followed Reliant's tried and tested recipe of a

The first car that was indigenous to Turkey came in the form of the FW5. Renamed as the Anadol, it was manufactured in Istanbul. *Thomas Touw*

fibreglass, two-door body attached to a steel chassis. Unlike other Reliants, this had recirculating ball steering instead of the usual rack-and-pinion setup and was powered by a 1,198cc (48.5bhp) Ford Cortina engine. The prototype was completed at Ogle Design Ltd in Letchworth, Hertfordshire and driven from there to Turkey.

Reliant offered the Koç organisation a 'package deal' in which it would do everything to get car production in Turkey up and running. This not only included supplying all drawings, moulds and jigs etc to build the vehicles but also employee training, factory design, specification of equipment, and plant layout. On 19 December 1966, the FW5 went into production at the Otosan plant in Istanbul and, following a competition to find a name for the new car, the name Anadol was chosen. Costing the equivalent of around £1,050, the Anadol was much cheaper than its mainstream competitors and so immediately found a very willing market. Initially, whilst the bodies were produced in Turkey, a number of the mechanical parts, including suspension units, steering, engine, gearbox and axle, were shipped to Turkey from Tamworth. The engine, gearbox and axle were procured from Ford by Reliant and then shipped out. Towards the end of 1967 the Anadol was so successful that the factory could not keep up with demand and so the factory was extended with a claimed 4,000 vehicles being built a year by 1968. For every vehicle built, Reliant was earning around £200 per car. In October 1968 the

engine was replaced with a more powerful 1,297cc Ford Kent engine, whilst 1969 saw a number of changes to the interior of the Anadol, with updated instrumentation and a more ergonomically designed steering wheel.

The Anadol was revised further in 1970 and, as such was renamed the Anadol 70. Externally, the round headlamps at the front were replaced by rectangular headlamps, along with new bumpers, whilst under the body a new transmission system was introduced. Production was such that in September 1970 the 10,000th Anadol was built and the waiting list for them was still around one year. Until now, the Anadol had only been available as a two-door version. However, in 1973 the model range was increased with the addition of a four-door saloon and estate version. Although Reliant assisted with testing a sports model called the Anadol STC-16 that was developed entirely in Turkey, Reliant's connection with Otosan started to ease off as Otasan became more independent with the Ford components now being supplied directly by a more-interested Ford, which paid Reliant a royalty per car — so high that as volumes grew beyond its expectations, Ford bought out the agreement, with a handsome one-off lump sum compensation, around 1976. Despite no further input from Reliant after the end of 1971, the Anadol continued to be developed and in a pickup form survived until 1991.

Cab & Crew Cab

With the sports car range and export models using Ford powertrain, Reliant had built up a strong working relationship with Ford that was to take a different route in 1965. Ford was looking at ways to produce a cab for the 'D' series of trucks for the overseas market. Not happy with the way other manufacturers built cabs with a single skinned wall made of thick laminates, Ford commissioned Reliant, which then developed and produced a prototype cab by May 1965. Similar to the Regal three-wheel body, it was made up of an outer and inner shell with a layer of air in between and weighed in 300lb lighter than a similar cab made from steel. After much testing, tweaking and following an evaluation programme, the cab was approved by Ford in July of the same year. The cab was designed in a way that it could be produced overseas in countries where a high duty was levied on sheet metal products. One of the first overseas companies to be set up for the production for Ford D-Type trucks was Otosan in Istanbul, Turkey in February 1966. Otosan were assembling both the Ford chassis and engine components in addition to manufacturing the fibreglass cabs. Reliant's body development engineer, Ken Wood visited Otosan for 17 days to teach workers how to produce and fit the cabs. Around three cabs were produced a day though ovens were not required to cure the fibreglass as the high temperature in the factory was sufficient to do so.

Reliant went on to break new ground in 1967 with the development of a Crew Cab for the Ford D-Truck that was capable of carrying up to six people and a driver. The Crew Cab featured a fully trimmed custom interior and could be converted to sleep two relief drivers for long-distance work. The cab was officially recognised by Ford and was included in its range of commercial vehicles. With a host of applications, numerous companies went on to use the cab including South Western Electricity Board and Merryweather & Sons Ltd, the manufacturer of fire fighting vehicles. It used the Crew Cab in its Marksman fire engine. Even Ford itself used the Crew Cab in its Competitions Department, building a customised car transporter to carry vehicles to races and rallies. The Crew Cab also caught the eye of Chrysler and, in 1974, Reliant produced a seven-man crew cab for the new Chrysler Commando commercial range of vehicles. The Crew Cab was restyled with a standard 'Commando' front end and was used on 7.38 to 16-ton vehicles.

Developed by Reliant, the fibreglass cab for the Ford D series truck was said to have been worth 'many millions of pounds' for the company.

Scooter Ski

Reliant was a company that was willing to pretty much adapt to anything and this was shown in 1967. The Scooter Ski was designed and patented by Tim Bedford, who then went on to form Scooter Ski Ltd in Draycott in Derbyshire. The craft itself was one of the forerunners for the modern jet ski and used a self-coloured fibreglass body that housed an Italian, air-cooled, 130cc (6bhp) Aspera two-stroke engine that was mounted in the body and drove a propeller at the rear. Fitted with handlebar steering that was attached to a rudder and a twist grip throttle, the Scooter Ski could comfortably skim across the water at speeds up to 20mph (32km/h). The engine was started via a self-winding recoil rope, using a centrifugal clutch that allowed it to remain stationary in the water.

Although Bedford had an office in Derbyshire, he had nowhere to build the craft and so approached Reliant, given the company's experience with fibreglass. Reliant agreed to build the new craft, with production starting in April 1967 with small batches of Scooter Skis being built. Scooter Ski Ltd handled the sales. Whilst orders in the UK were, as expected, quite small, it did find a willing market abroad and, by 1969, a new version, called the Hunter, was introduced. This was now fitted with a more powerful 185cc Rotax single-cylinder, light alloy engine that was able to run for 5.5 hours on 2.5 gallons of petrol. The Hunter also featured minor

The Scooter Ski was designed by Scooter Ski Ltd and subsequently developed and manufactured by Reliant.

modifications to the body; this was now slightly wider, giving the craft a beam of 3ft 6in and staying at eight feet in length. The Hunter also included the addition of a small Perspex windscreen.

Costing around £269 ex-works each, the first batch of 2,500 craft was dispatched by Reliant to Nouveau Products Corporation in the USA. This was then followed by a further 1,000 craft being sent to Italy and Sweden. Following the 1970 International Boat Show in London, export orders for over £700,000 were taken for the Scooter Ski with American police forces also showing an interest in them for

patrolling rivers and harbours. Along with numerous other orders including a £400,000 order for 1,500 Scooter Skis for the PMF Marine Division of Ted Stainbrook Inc in California, the value of overseas orders for the period between 1970 and 1973 amounted to around £1,200,000. Success was short-lived, however, as by the early 1970s, rival companies were now building craft with jet propulsion and in greater volumes. This led to many orders for the Scooter Ski being cancelled and sales started to tail off, leaving Reliant with a huge stock of redundant components.

TW9

In its early days, Reliant had offered commercial vehicles with various payloads as Tom Williams firmly believed that there was a market for such vehicles. However, as the Reliant vehicle range developed the commercial range shrank down to just a 5cwt van. One profitable relationship that Reliant had built up was with Mediterranean Engine Brand Enterprises Association (MEBEA) in Greece, who initially placed an order for 150 left-hand-drive Reliant Regal Super Saloons followed by just over 400 of the 3,000 10cwt pick-ups built in 1966. For Reliant, this amounted to almost £200,000 of orders, so when MEBEA mentioned that it wanted a vehicle that was capable of a much larger capacity, Reliant undertook market research that showed there was also a market for such a vehicle in the home market. Reliant started to develop a new vehicle, code named TW9, with a myth that the first prototype was built in just four days; however, in reality it took longer.

The TW9 was a 16cwt (800kg) payload pick-up truck that was much larger than any other previous Reliant three-wheeler at 12ft 3in long, 4ft 11in wide and 5ft 10in high. The chassis was a basic ladder frame arrangement with the steering almost identical to the Regal and power coming from the 701cc Reliant engine producing 29.5bhp. At the time Reliant had already started developing the TW8 (that would become the Reliant Robin), and as Ogle was involved in this project, Reliant asked Tom Karen to come up with a fibreglass cab for the TW9. This he did with a cab that featured flat sides and a long sloping front. Whilst looking familiar to present-day eyes, in the 1960s it was the complete opposite of the standard body designs that were in use at that time. Furthermore, unlike most vehicles, there was no exterior access to the engine bay. Instead the Spartan interior, with fibreglass-moulded seats, had a canopy over the engine that was easily accessed from inside the cab.

Designed primarily for the export market, initially the Mediterranean and the Middle East, its launch in September 1967 coincided with an order from MEBEA for 250 vehicles. By April 1968, 450 TW9s had been shipped to Greece, bringing in sales totalling £200,000 for Reliant and by November in the same year, the total had reached 800 vehicles, the contract raking in half a million pounds over fourteen months. Despite its initial success and indeed the handsome profit margin, the TW9 was finding life in the Mediterranean difficult for, although it had been specifically designed to operate in harsh conditions, it was soon discovered that the 701cc engine could not cope with extremely mountainous terrain when carrying a full load. Consequently, from early 1968, the 1,200cc

Provided in its base form as a chassis cab, the TW9 was then converted into numerous forms.

A batch of TW9s ready for delivery outside MEBEA factory headquarters in Greece.

(39bhp) Triumph Herald engine was sourced and fitted to all examples purchased by MEBEA, and identified as the TW9-B keeping the 16cwt payload. Now deciding to build and assemble the vehicles itself, in December 1968 MEBEA placed an order for 500 TW9-Bs in a CKD format that again brought in another £175,000 for Reliant.

The TW9 also went on sale in the UK though only with the 701cc engine with the TW9-B models being for export only. Whilst available from Reliant with a pick-up type body that had a wooden pick-up type back with drop down sides, other versions of the TW9 were now starting to appear. One of the more notable conversions was the

Above: A vehicle belonging to Harvey & Co Leeds Ltd displays the carrying capacity of the TW9, with a Regal 3/35 saloon on board. *Ian McLoughlin*

Left: Amongst many other organisations, the TW9 was used by a number of local councils for a variety of tasks, from road sweeping to refuse collection.

Melford-Reliant Suction Sweeper created by Melford Engineering in Cambridge. Melford took the TW9 and created a road sweeper version with a 12cwt hopper with suction fans and brushes being powered by a second Reliant 701cc engine attached to the vehicle. Another version was the 'Minibug' created by the Ray Smith Co, which designed a concept whereby the bodies of the TW9 could be easily swapped. This allowed the owner of a TW9 greater flexibility by being able to convert it from, for example, a pick-up truck to a side-loading refuse truck. Ray Smith also built a road sweeper similar to that created by Melford Engineering, called the 'Streetwalker'; this was sold through BTB Equipment Sales in Lancashire. With reference to the Minibug, Ray Smith stated in *Commercial Motor* that:

> 'Whenever we sold one of these bugs we would go to Tamworth to collect them and all the delivery drivers were expected to carry a house brick. The reason for this was that the accelerator pedal was so high off the floor that any journey over five miles was absolute torture for the driver unless he could rest his foot on a brick!'

In 1973 the engine in the TW9 was changed for the 748cc unit and, although the 848cc engine was introduced in 1975, it was not available in the TW9 until February 1978. The latter was said to provide a top speed of 55mph (88km/h) unladen, although it was much slower when fully laden, and offered a fuel consumption of 35mpg (8.1 litre/100km).

Ant

Whilst the TW9 had gained a number of nicknames it was not until 1975 that it also became the Ant when BTB Equipment Sales started to build its own bodies. It created a number of vehicles called the Ant that were designed to fill niche markets; these included an aluminium panel van and a 'hi-tip' skip loader. In 1977 BTB Equipment Sales contacted Reliant asking if it could buy the rights to the TW9 that would also include the drawings, moulds and jigs used to create it. As we shall see later in the book, by 1977 Reliant was still recovering from the 1974 miners' strike and the three-day week that followed. Consequently, as the TW9 was not one of its major concerns and had had very little development since its introduction, Reliant agreed to sell in May 1978. This helped generate extra income for Reliant as, whilst BTB built the cabs and bodies, Reliant continued to build the chassis and running gear, supplying these to BTB. The TW9 was now officially renamed the Ant, with around 400 vehicles a year being made, half of these being for the export market, with the remainder being used by a number of companies, including local authorities. One Ant also found its way to the Balmoral Royal estate in Aberdeenshire, where it was used as an all-purpose vehicle around the grounds. In some cases, where a heavy duty Ant was required, the Reliant engine was found to be underpowered in certain situations and so BTB also supplied an Ant with a Chrysler/Talbot Avenger engine. In 1982, BTB sold the rights of the Ant to an American company called Dunn, which moved production of the vehicles to Oswaldtwistle in Lancashire, where the Ant was then renamed as the Antruck, though being built in the same formats as before. By now, the UK market was being saturated with small four-wheel commercial vehicles from Japan and so, as sales of the Antruck declined, Dunn sold the rights in 1986 to the Hutson Motor Co in Bradford; however, no further vehicles were produced.

The Ant, seen here with a low loading body and 12in drop sides and tailboards. This particular vehicle was used by the City of Stoke on Trent Parks and Recreation department in Hanley Park.

Onwards and Upwards

As detailed earlier, whilst the Reliant three-wheeler pretty much had no real competition in the market, its nearest rival was Bond Cars Ltd in Preston, Lancashire which, (formerly under the name of Sharps Commercials) had been producing three-wheel cars since 1949. These, however, were light mini-cars with small engines and not quite in the same league as the Reliant Regal until Bond released the Bond 875 in 1965. Like the Regal, this was a much more car-like vehicle, powered with an all alloy 850cc Hillman Imp engine. However, it suffered numerous teething problems that delayed its availability to the public and financially hit Bond badly. With a restyled Bond 875 Mk II version in 1968, the Bond 875 was selling slowly; the company's biggest seller was the Equipe four-wheeled sports car that had been introduced in 1963. Designed by

Lawrie Bond, the Equipe used a running chassis from the Triumph Herald and was powered by the Triumph Spitfire's 1,147cc engine. Furthermore the close association with Triumph also had the advantage that the Bond Equipe was sold through Triumph dealers. In 1964 a more powerful 1,296cc engine was fitted and this was changed again to a 2-litre Triumph Vitesse engine in 1967, with the introduction of more refined Equipe 2.

Way ahead of its time and predating similar designs like the Lotus Esprit and Fiat X19, the FW7 (also dubbed Rogue 700) was created in 1969. Using the Reliant engine, just one running example was built.
Tom Karen

Bond Cars Ltd (whilst it was still Sharps Commercials) had been bought by Loxham's Garages, which was part of the Bradshaw Group. In 1968 the Bradshaw Group decided to sell Loxham's Garages (including Bond's premises) to the Dutton Forshaw Group. As a result a buyer was required for the manufacturing activities of Bond, as Bond Cars Ltd, itself. At the time the Bond management was unable to raise the necessary capital and so approached both Triumph and then Hodge Finance. Triumph was not interested, although following the nod from British Leyland Motor Corporation Ltd's George Turnbull, Reliant was, on the basis that the Scimitar could join the Equipe in having access to Triumph dealers. Reliant became the new owners of Bond Cars Ltd in February 1969, leasing the actual Preston premises from Dutton Forshaw; however, after the acquisition, Donald Stokes from BLMC pulled the plug on the tacit agreement.

Despite how it may have seemed with Reliant buying up the competition, there were no real threat from Bond that could hamper Reliant's sales. In 1969, Reliant was producing 15,000 three wheelers a year and employed over 1,600 employees across its three sites, whilst Bond produced 1,500 three-wheelers a year and had 300 employees. For Reliant, the Bond Equipe looked very lucrative business as with it came access to numerous Triumph dealers up and down the country. In addition, as the Equipe mainly used Triumph parts, there were no expensive redesigns to consider and the Equipe's fibreglass body produced no issues at all for a company that was a grand master with such material. Reliant started to upgrade the Equipe (now codenamed FW8); this initially continued to use Triumph components but with a grand plan that eventually, Reliant would engineer and use its own. It was soon realised that the Preston site was not suitable for volume production of the FW8 and the Tamworth site was already working at full capacity with several profitable models. The FW8 project was, therefore, quietly dropped as Reliant could not commit fully to it.

Reliant kept hold of Bond's premises in Preston, where workers continued to manufacture the Bond 875 to fulfil existing orders. As Bond had also produced its own version of the Scooter Ski, production of the Reliant version was also moved to the Preston factory. This was then followed in June 1970 by the Bond Bug; however, following alleged production and quality problems along with the economics of running two similar production lines, Reliant closed the site down in December 1970. Everything was then moved to its Tamworth site. Bond Cars Ltd had thus became a subsidiary of the Reliant Motor Group.

FW7

Reliant looked into designing a small mid-engined sports car in 1969. Code named FW7, the sports car used Reliant's economy drivetrain from the three-wheel range. The design, although similar to the Fiat X19, actually predated the Fiat by two years. Reliant built a mock-up of the car in 1970 but it was soon realised that the Reliant engine would not be powerful enough for the vehicle and so the project was terminated.

Rogue to Bond Bug

Just before Reliant acquired Bond Cars Ltd, the former had been looking at a new 'fun' three-wheeler that was the brainchild of Tom Karen at Ogle Design. Even before being commissioned by Reliant, Karen had long had an idea to create such a vehicle with his first attempt being a small two-seat vehicle called the Vimp built by him and Andrew Waddicor in 1954. Four years later, Karen won a national car design competition with a new concept three-wheeler called the Rascal of which Karen states:

> 'It was a model of simplicity; the body was made up of a few parts, each one could come out of a mould without undercuts — obviating the need to bolt and unbolt moulds. The main shell stretched from the nose to the back and comprised the floor and seats. There was only one door (one set of hinges, one lock, one fitting time) with a flat windscreen and one wiper. The soft screens could be removed and in the event of a roll over, made escape easy.'

Reliant had historically built commercial and family three-wheelers and so, whilst Ogle was involved in the overall design, its cars were very much designed for a purpose rather than for fun. Interested in the idea of a three-wheeler that was both sporting and fun, Ray Wiggin asked Karen to produce more drawings, though stating that the overall design must include as many existing Reliant parts as possible.

During 1968, Ogle created a mock-up of the vehicle and seeing it, Reliant ordered it to build a prototype even though Reliant were not sure if the company would put it into production or not. Provisionally called the Rogue, a prototype was created; this featured a fibreglass body and a profile formed of a right-angled triangle with manually operated round pop-up headlights. Access was gained by lifting up a canopy that almost comprised the entire top half of the car. The body had moulded in seats and no doors, with each side being open, whilst the back of the vehicle was cropped, exposing the rear axle. Although the front used a similar steering and suspension system to the Regal, the rear was quite different — fitted with vertical coil spring and damper units, along

The Reliant Rogue prototype built in 1968 before it was developed further into the Bond Bug. *Tom Karen*

with a large anti-roll bar. Powered by Reliant's 701cc engine, the chassis was a modified version of the TW8 (Robin) that was currently being designed by John Crosthwaite. Upon completion of the first prototype in 1969, Reliant codenamed the project TW11 and then requested that a number of changes were made as the company felt the pop-up headlights were too expensive and added unnecessary extra weight. It also asked that a provision be made for a small luggage area behind the seats; however, whilst being a sensible move, this made the body more complicated to make. A second prototype was created; this had fixed headlamps and also incorporated other updates, like cluster lights, fitted into the body and a flat windscreen that used a single wiper blade. A hatch was also added to the rear of the Rogue; this was accessed via a small drop down wooden door. At this point Reliant was unsure of what to do and whether such a vehicle should bear the Reliant name.

The takeover of Bond Cars in 1969 immediately answered the company's question. Partially on account of its claimed top speed, the Bond 875 had appealed to a younger audience. Bond had also used its name with great advantage during an era where the cinema was extremely popular and Ian Fleming's fictional spy, James Bond, was often top of the bill. Whilst never referring to the actual character itself, Bond's advertising for the Equipe sports car often carried brand lines along the lines of, 'Sorry – no ejector seat' and 'To James with love'. The Bond name, therefore, hinted at being both adventurous and fun and so it seemed the ideal one with which to launch the new Rogue. That said the name Bond Rogue just did not roll off the tongue and so the vehicle was renamed the Bond Bug.

Tom Karen proposed that only one colour was used and complemented with bold graphics. Therefore, only one colour — tangerine — was available! With the Rascal being lime green, this colour was also considered for the Bug and a few promotional vehicles for Rose's Cordials were produced in lime green (along with several white Bugs for Cape Fruit and Rothmans' Tobacco). It was found that green was actually much more expensive to produce than tangerine,; the latter also made the Bugs highly visible, and so that became the standard colour. Another first for Reliant was that the Bug featured vinyl decals rather than the metal badges that had been used on previous Reliants and which were the norm for many other cars of that era.

The Bond Bug was launched at Woburn Abbey on 7 June 1970 and as planned was aimed at the 17 to 25 age group. It was offered in three versions, the 700 (priced at £548 0s 4d), being a 'stripped out' economy model with hardly anything as standard equipment and fitted with the 29bhp 701cc engine straight out of the Regal 3/30. The 700E (costing £579 7s 0d), which had full weather equipment 'styling refinements' consisting of side-screens, heater, demister, sun visors and several other additions, along with the 29bhp engine. At the top of the range was the 700ES with a price tag of £628 19s 2d that incorporated all the benefits of the 700E, along with a high-compression version of the 701cc engine, developing 31bhp and additional features, including Goodyear Decathlon bias-belted low profile tyres and mudflaps at the rear. With the high-compression engine, Reliant claimed that the 700ES was capable of 0-60mph (0-96km/h) in 19 seconds and a top speed of over 70mph (113km/h). The young market it was aimed at, however, was probably less interested in knowing that it could also achieve 73mpg (3.9-litre/100km) at a constant 30mph (48km/h).

Production began with the Bug being assembled at the Preston site, with many of the materials and components shipped from Reliant's other sites (fibreglass body sections from Kettlebrook and most mechanical parts from Shenstone). It is alleged that a number of conflicts between Reliant and Bond staff arose and that fibreglass bodies made at the Kettlebrook site were reaching Preston with defects, which then had to be addressed before the vehicles could be assembled. In turn, this meant that production targets were not being met and, combined with the economics of running the Bond factories, resulted in their closure as part of a bid to rationalise production, with all equipment being moved to Tamworth.

Although it was the most expensive version, by August 1970, the 700ES was outselling the 700E at the rate of six-to-one, whilst at the other end of the spectrum there had been no demand at all for the basic 700 version, with only a single pre-production car known to have been produced (in May 1970).

Above: Whilst Reliant could not guarantee that three Bond Bugs could be parked at any meter, it was possible in a few places in London's West End where spaces were larger than usual. The image also won a poster design award in 1972.

Right: The Bond Bug was aimed at the 17-25-year-old age group and as such was advertised as a fun vehicle. This 1970 poster further enhances that with reference to '2 aircraft seats' and a 'Lift-up aircraft-type cockpit cover'.

The distinctive shape of the Bond Bug was very well received; this helped to boost its publicity as it appeared in numerous magazines, newspapers and TV programmes. With the arrival of the 1970 Motor Show at Earl's Court in London, it seemed that Reliant would not be able to publicise its latest addition further, as at that time, SMMT rules still stated that three-wheelers were classed as tricycles and thus not eligible to be displayed at the show. It was then the brain wave of Reliant's Marketing Manager, Roger Musgrave, to create a 'Double Bug' by combing two Bugs back to back to create a four-wheeler, the wheels being arranged in a rhomboidal layout. Now a four-wheeler, the Double Bug was placed on Reliant's stand and adorned with ladies dressed as 'Bug Bunnies'. A large sign was hung above it proclaiming: 'Sorry you can't buy this Bug, but we'll sell you half of it.' Despite confusing some visitors to the show, it was a great success, and afterwards was lent to numerous Reliant dealers as part of an ongoing publicity campaign.

Below: Built for the 1970 Earl's Court Motor Show, the Double Bug was made by joining two Bond Bugs together back-to-back so it had four wheels and thus was eligible to enter the show. It is seen here back at Reliant shortly after the show. *Clive Stanley*

Left: The wedge shaped profile of the Bond Bug and a back end that Reliant referred to as a 'chopped off' look. *Ron Biggin*

Below: With no doors, access to the Bond Bug was via an upward opening canopy, as it was envisaged that youthful drivers and passengers would be scrambling in and out through the large openings on either side. *Ron Biggin*

Despite the initial flurry of sales at its launch, towards the end of 1971 sales of the Bug had reduced to around 20 vehicles a week and Reliant looked at whether it should change its policy of only offering the Bug in tangerine only to help boost its appeal. Four out of seven of Reliant's area sales managers believed that more colours should be introduced; however, after running a survey amongst Bug owners and dealers, less than 2% of owners believed that a colour choice was needed and just 15% of dealers thought the Bug should be offered in more than one colour. It, therefore, continued in one colour only.

The 700ES version still remained the most popular choice and in 1972, 416 of this model were sold compared with 33 of the 700E. By October 1973, the Bug became the 750E and 750ES, when it was fitted with the new 748cc engine that was being specified for the Robin. Just 142 750 versions had been produced, when in May 1974, the Bug was discontinued in order to provide more production capacity for the Robin. In total, 2,268 Bugs had been built; however, interest in it remained long after the last Bug rolled off the production line.

Scimitar GTE SE5

Whilst the Scimitar GT was a success for Reliant, the interior was not exceptionally spacious and although it had four seats it was only really suitable for two adults with two children in the back or three adults with the third adult sprawled across the rear seat. Reliant had acknowledged this and explored whether the Scimitar GT could be extended into a true four-seater with plenty of luggage space. Once again engaging Tom Karen at Ogle Design Ltd, Karen came up with a number of ideas which also included extending the rear of Scimitar GT Coupé body shell and using a rising waistline/roofline (referred to by Karen as an extended greenhouse). Karen believed that, rather than expand the Scimitar GT into a large version, it was better to create a new model from scratch that retained as many of the original features as possible. Before long, in September 1967 Ogle set about creating a full sized mock-up of the proposed GTE (Grand Turismo Estate), in which Tom Karen admits: 'I stuck my neck out with quite a radical proposal; a sporting estate car.'

During its development, Ray Wiggin visited Ogle and, spotting the new GTE, was so taken by its shape that he gave the project the go-ahead with no further questions and rejected the extended Scimitar GT version. Ogle Design then created a GTE prototype in its studios at Letchworth and, when completed, drove the GTE to Reliant in Tamworth for evaluation in January 1968. As the GTE was longer than the Scimitar GT, Reliant's Chief Engineer, John Crosthwaite, set about engineering a completely new chassis. This included outriggers and perpendicular rails that offered greater side impact protection. Although a new model, the GTE did manage to use the doors, windscreen and bumper from the Scimitar GT. Well before hatchback vehicles were the norm, the GTE body also incorporated a feature pretty much unique for its time in the form of a top-hinged rear window that, in early models, was supported by a spring arm; this was later replaced by gas struts. Tom Karen also notes that:

'Apart from pioneering the sporting estate formula, the waist line of the GTE went up all the way to the back. Many people found this hard to swallow, but this feature has found its way on every car designed since then (with notable exceptions; Rolls Royce and top end Mercedes cars), The long roof, apart from providing interior space, was very beneficial.'

Inside, the GTE had a similar dashboard to that fitted in the Scimitar

The Scimitar GTE prototype that left Ogle in January 1968. The front end was likened to the Ogle Mini with four headlamps behind a wire mesh. Ogle Design were asked to change the headlamps, though the body was left unchanged. *RSSOC*

GT but, more importantly, it had four large arm chairs, two in the front and two in the back, each separated by an arm rest. The rear seats folded down providing ample luggage space in the rear and, in addition, the rear armrest hinged forward when the seats were folded flat, stopping luggage sliding forward into the cockpit area. Delighted with the prototype, Wiggin requested several changes, including a restyled front nose and grille, modifying rear ventilation and fitting 14in wheels, before finally making the decision that the GTE was ready to go into full scale production

In October 1968, the new Scimitar GTE (SE5) appeared at the Motor Show in London and the first ever sporting estate car was born. Initially, feedback on the GTE was very mixed and was pretty much like a jar of Marmite in that some people loved it and some hated it. Whatever the views, once a number of journalists took the GTE out on road tests many were very impressed with its capabilities. The Scimitar GTE was the only production car on the market at the time that offered high cruising speeds, could seat four adults in comfort and had luggage space as well. Powered by a 2,994cc Ford Essex engine that produced 136bhp, the Scimitar had a top speed approaching 120mph (193km/h) and was priced at £1,759 including Purchase Tax plus an additional £64 for an overdrive unit. As a result, it became very desirable and Reliant's profile was raised significantly during the life of the GTE, as it became the car of choice for numerous celebrities, including Barry Sheen, Ken Dodd, Noel Edmonds and Graham Hill.

The is the very first Reliant the author recalls seeing whilst at boarding school in 1977: a Scimitar GTE SE5. It belongs to one of the school's teachers, Bob Cole, and at the time was noted with amusement for its 'plastic' body. The last laugh, however, is with Bob Cole as, all these years later, he still owns and uses it.

A Scimitar GTE SE5 being crash tested at the Motor Industry Research Association (MIRA) in 1968.

This particular shot of a Scimitar GTE with the Royal Air Force Red Arrows swooping low over it, was promoted by the *Sunday Express* as one of the most striking advertising photographs in 1970.

Also on show at the 1968 Motorshow was a unique version of the Scimitar GTE created by Ogle Design Ltd and built for Sir Julian Hodge's wife. Along with Ogle logos embossed into the front wings, the car had electric windows, electric retractable headlamp covers and a glazed roof section. The interior was furnished in light tan with leather and chequered fabric seats.

Ogle Design Ltd said:

'The new and exciting 3 litre Scimitar by Ogle, based on the Reliant GTE, incorporates a number of extra features which give this new concept car an even more futuristic look. Apart from the large windscreen and glass roof over the front seats the most striking difference is the frontal grille area. The Ogle Scimitar has a concealed headlamp system which embodies four of the new Lucas 'all-glass' rectangular sealed beam units, with electrically operated shutters. These 60/60 watt light units are a result of two years development work, and offer all the advantages already associated with the sealed beam principle. When

In 1967 Ogle produced a one-off luxury experimental GTE seen here with Mrs Hodge. Externally one of the most striking features was a concealed headlamp system with electrically operated shutters.

the headlamp shutters are closed, the light units are fully protected and the full frontal area of the car has a flowing and distinctive appearance.'

Following the show, the Ogle Scimitar GTE was passed over to Lady Moira Hodge and it was still owned by the Hodge family until 2014, when it appeared on the Internet for sale.

The biggest accolade for the new Scimitar GTE came in 1970, when Princess Anne was spotted driving a GTE in London. The car had been loaned to Her Royal Highness by the Kenning Group as a trial and it must have made a favourable impression, as shortly afterwards, Reliant received an order for a new GTE from Buckingham Palace. The vehicle was then presented to Princess Anne as a combined 20th birthday/Christmas present from HM Queen Elizabeth II and other members of the Royal family. The Royal GTE was a SE5 finished in Aircraft Blue and trimmed in grey leather. It was registered 1420 H, which reflected Princess Anne's position as Colonel-in-Chief of the Royal 14/20th Hussars. The GTE offered the Princess high-speed motoring and it had plenty of room for her horse-riding equipment. Princess Anne formed a great bond with the Scimitar and went on to own another eight GTEs and a Middlebridge Scimitar.

Whilst harmony may have settled on the Scimitar production line, things were very different at the Ford Motor Co. In January 1971, having rejected a £2 increase on their wages, workers walked out of Ford's Dagenham, Halewood and Swansea plants. This, in turn, had a knock-on effect with GTE production as Reliant was no longer being supplied with the Ford V6 engine. Production continued as normal until the sixth week of the Ford strike when the company slowed down to building the cars just three days a week — with no engines. It wasn't until May 1971 that Reliant was able to start building GTEs at the rate of 30 vehicles a week again; however, by this time 250 vehicles had been lost as a result of the strike. During the same year, Reliant also introduced its 'common sense price policy', which set out to eliminate the abundance of optional extras that the motoring industry tended to add on to vehicles to help expand the basic purchase price. With this in mind, Reliant introduced two versions of the Scimitar GTE that included its extras as standard: the Scimitar GTE Overdrive and the Scimitar GTE Automatic. The former had a four-speed box with LH type Laycock overdrive unit as standard, along with a heated rear screen. After a number of complaints from the press saying how dirty the rear screen got, a rear screen wash/wiper (another Reliant first). The overdrive version was priced at £1,743.50 (£2,278.53 with Purchase Tax), whilst the automatic version, which was fitted with a Borg & Warner unit, was priced at £1,811.00 (£2,366.65 with Purchase Tax).

Princess Anne leaving Buckingham Palace in 1970 with a loaned Scimitar GTE that was made available by Reliant through the Kenning Motor Group. *RSSOC*

The Scimitar GTE assembly line; at this point the chassis and running gear have been assembled and the body is being lowered into place.
Thomas Touw

replaced; this, along with a new carburettor, increased the bhp from 138 to 145 and gave the car a top speed of 125mph (201km/h). In 1972, sales of the GTE had increased by 58% and were continuing to climb, such was its success. In the same year the Reliant Sabre & Scimitar Owner's club was also formed by Robin Rew.

The GTE received more modifications for 1974 in order to produce a more executive type Scimitar. These changes included rear seat belts and quartz halogen headlights. However, Scimitar GTE production was hit again by industrial action from 1 January to 7 March 1974 as a result of a coal miners' strike, though Reliant was able to resume full production again from 8 March 1974. Towards the end of the year, as a result of the economic climate, demand for the Scimitar GTE had declined considerably, with the long waiting list for the vehicle being dramatically shortened as a result. Perhaps as a consequence of this, in conjunction with Hodge Finance, Reliant offered a special 9.5% interest finance scheme for all versions of the Scimitar GTE and the three-wheel Robin van that ran from December 1974 to January 1975. This compared with the average 16.5% interest schemes that were in place with other cars in the UK. Things looked very different just eight months later when registrations of the GTE grew by 9.7% in a year with August 1975 seeing an all-time record for the GTE with 248 new registrations.

SE6

Reliant continued to improve the GTE and, in October 1972, it gave the model a revamp; it was now termed the SE5a. The makeover included a slightly higher nose cone, which raised the height of the front lights, and a new grille. New Scimitar shield logo badges were added to the side of the front wings, new door handles, the chrome strip along the side was removed and a new set of lights at the rear now included reversing lights in the cluster. The rear lamp cluster was a breakthrough for Reliant. For the first time it could justify laying down new tooling, jointly with Lotus, which specified it for the company's new Elite. The tooling investment with Lucas was shared pro-rata to each company's anticipated sales volumes. Jensen was later to use the same rear lamp; however, its inflated volume expectations for the Jensen-Healey, to which it was fitted, resulted in a welcome bonus rebate to both Reliant and Lotus! The interior was also revamped with a new vacuum formed ABS plastic fascia using a laminated sheet, newly developed by ICI, that provided a soft-feel skin of leather look-alike material; this was fitted with new rocker switches (instead of the older style toggle switches) and new warning lights for various functions. Along with numerous other additions, like foot well vents to improve ventilation, seat belts were now also fitted as standard. The engine in the SE5a was also slightly improved upon with the inlet manifold being

Ray Wiggin was well aware of the criticism thrown at the GTE for having a cramped interior space; however, it was following Princess Anne's newest order that he wished to provide a GTE for her that had more legroom behind the front seats. So, in 1974, he initiated a development programme, led by Ken Wood, head of Reliant's body engineering team, to look into increasing the leg room. In order to define what dimensions would be suitable, Wood and his team cut a SE5 body shell in half, in line with the rear door opening, and set about inserting 4in extra into the wheel base and making the doors 2.5in longer. Tom Karen of Ogle Design was again engaged to restyle a new longer and wider GTE whilst, at the same time, keeping the distinctive look of the SE5 series. The end result was a much sleeker GTE, dubbed the SE6, with a body that was around 4in longer and 3in wider, giving the car increased interior space with both extra legroom and elbow space.

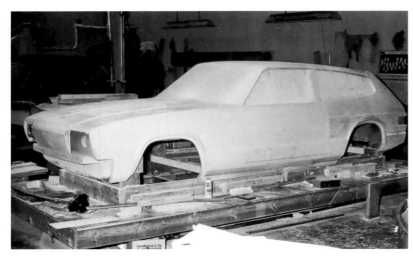

Left: In order to create the larger Scimitar SE6, a Scimitar SE5 body shell was cut longitudinally down the centre and, once widened, cut in half ahead of the B-pillar and then lengthened.

Below: Visually identical to the Scimitar SE6, the SE6a featured stiffer suspension and improved brakes. *Dave Poole*

This particular Scimitar GTE SE6a, seen here with false number plates and bonnet mascot, is believed to be one of the Scimitars previously owned by Princess Anne. *Dave Poole*

Externally, the SE6 was instantly recognisable by its larger twin headlights, black moulded polyurethane bumpers, the removal of the quarter light windows and the replacement of the expensive chrome plated brass finishers by more affordable Jaguar-style chrome iron sections.

The interior was also completely redesigned with a new black fascia moulding that incorporated a number of proprietary Smiths instruments, including a cluster shared with Triumph. The seats were also more luxurious and more substantial, being trimmed in nylon with leather-cloth sides and backs, thus helping the SE6 appeal to the executive market. These changes were coupled with increased sound proofing and numerous features now added as standard; these included electric windows, aerial, internal adjusted door mirrors and rear seat belts. Optional extras included leather trim and power

steering as well as a Phillips RN 642 stereo radio and cassette player. Using the same engine as the SE5, the SE6 made its debut at the Earl's Court Motor Show in 1975 and its design was such that Reliant pulled in £3 million worth of orders from the show. It came in two versions: the Overdrive version for £4,367.61 and the Automatic for £4,446.00 (both prices including Car Tax and VAT).

After the SE6 was launched, it was soon realised that the new design had created problems with the front suspension settings, as the front springs and dampers were too soft causing complaints of bottoming and sluggish handling. Reliant responded to this by fitting uprated Girling units and changed units on existing cars under warranty. Although the SE6 was more civilised than its predecessor and much better for long-distance touring with a larger fuel tank, a number of other niggles were also being reported; these included the

Ritchie Spencer (left) discussing matters with works manager, Richard Whittington, on the Scimitar GTE SE6b production line.

European contacts to establish a European export network. This was a very successful programme and, by August of the same year, the Scimitar was being sold in Austria, Switzerland, Belgium, Holland, Greece and the Faroe Islands. In the home market however the Scimitar was not selling as well as it had and following the J F Nash take-over in summer 1977, production was cut back. Initially, all future development was halted; however, in 1980, Ford discontinued the 3-litre V6 Essex engine, replacing it with the German-built 2.8-litre Cologne engine. Reliant, therefore, had little choice but to modify the SE6a to get the engine into it with the vehicle then becoming the SE6b in the same year. Although the new engine had similar power to the old model, it had a lower torque, which meant reduced performance. To compensate, Reliant had to reduce the ratio in the rear axle to help boost performance. Due to the size of the engine a number of modifications were required under the bonnet which included a redesigned cooling system. Externally, the SE6b also had a mild make-over with the nose cleaned up and stripped of lettering and chrome strips, both being replaced by a single shield-shape badge. To help increase the model's appeal and retain an executive feel, each came with electric mirrors, intermittent wipers, halogen headlamps, rear fog lights, seatbelt warning light and rubber door strips. An electric sunroof was also available as an optional extra. The interior was also improved, with a choice of several new upholstery colours, whilst still retaining the Scimitar's impressive luggage space, which increased from 20cu ft to 40cu ft with both the individual rear seats folded down. In 1981 the longevity of the SE6b was further increased with the introduction of galvanised chassis that was then fitted to all vehicles.

power steering being too light, body flexing and doors dropping on their hinges. After just 1,550 SE6 models were built, Reliant addressed all these issues in late 1976 with the SE6a. Although this was virtually identical externally, the chassis was now much stiffer and suspension settings were modified to improve handling. In addition, although there had been no complaints concerning the brakes, the braking system was improved and now fitted with Lockheed 10in brake drums on the rear instead of Girling 9in drums and disc brakes at the front.

Reliant anticipated that 1977 would be the most significant yet for the Scimitar with a new export programme being launched for the SE6a and so it increased production from 35 vehicles a week to 50 vehicles with the introduction of a night shift. Jaguar's chairman, F R W ('Lofty') England had retired to live in Austria, so Ray Wiggin and former Jaguar apprentice, Barrie Wills, persuaded him to use his

With the arrival of the 1980s, the recession that had hit Britain at that time was starting to bite, and sales of the Scimitar had decreased dramatically with just two to three cars being built a week in 1981. This continued until 1985 when it was announced that production of the Scimitar was to cease. The Scimitar managed to limp on until November 1986 with the company building Scimitars to order before the last GTE left the production line and was sent on its way to Princess Anne, making this her seventh and final Reliant-manufactured Scimitar.

Expansion for the 1970s

With the arrival of the 1970s the Reliant Motor Co was at the very height of its success, its turnover constantly averaging over £20,000,000. Its Scimitar sports cars were hitting record sales whilst production of three-wheelers was running at record highs, with around 300 Regal Saloons and Supervans rolling off the assembly line each week. In addition export sales of all Reliant vehicles was raking money in from all around the world. Indeed, Greece and Turkey owed practically their entire motor industries to Reliant's 'package deal' plan. With so many fingers in so many pies, it was little wonder that Reliant was the UK's second most profitable motor manufacturer in 1971 and 1972. At this point in time Reliant was also Tamworth's largest employer with over 1,800 employees.

In order to build on its success, in 1972 Reliant embarked on a £1,750,000 three-year expansion scheme to increase its factory space by two and a half times from 97,000sq ft to 242,000sq ft. The scheme not only created more space for Reliant but also more jobs, potentially increasing the number of employees to 2,500. Given the proximity of the site to local homes, Reliant allocated a further £50,000 to excavation and other work to help ensure all buildings

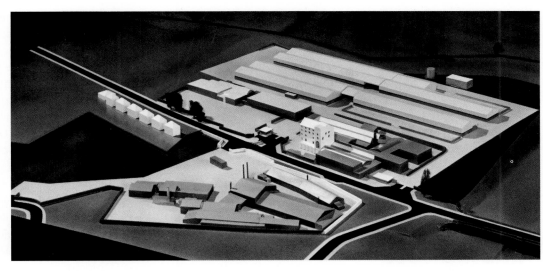

This model shows just how big Reliant's expansion proposals were in 1972 with the company spreading out on both sides of the A5.

had a low profile and blended in with the surroundings with the design and construction of the buildings being undertaken by IDC Ltd of Stratford-upon-Avon. The new buildings saw a completely new paint shop and assembly line for the upcoming Robin. All three-wheel vehicle production was shifted from the north side of the A5 to the new assembly hall. The old assembly shops were then used for service work and various other operations. Whilst the new Robin hall fell under Stage 1 of Reliant's development program, under Stage 2 there was a prospect of a second hall for the Scimitar GTE. This awaited further investment funding from Saab (see Saab Sonett), which never arrived as the project did not go ahead.

Construction of the Robin assembly hall in 1971.

The site at Kettlebrook — the fibreglass moulding plant — was also to be doubled in size from 70,000sq ft to 131,000sq ft whilst the site at Shenstone — engine, gearbox, axles etc — was to receive an 'extensive modernisation programme'. This included a new parts warehouse in 1973; this was positioned by the Shenstone factory and contained 9,000 different items covering all Reliant models. From here parts were despatched to 16 regional distributors, which then fed Reliant dealers. With over 100,000 Reliant vehicles on the road, sales of Reliant parts at this point in time were worth £2 million a year and, to help maintain sales, a 'R-parts' symbol was introduced; this was attached to all spare parts. Genuine Reliant parts had a 12-month warranty and were of the same quality as the original to discourage owners buying cheaper imitations.

Saab Sonett

The Saab Sonett was a sports car manufactured by Saab Automobile AB of Sweden between 1955 and 1957, before going back into production in 1966. Whilst the Sonett passed through various model changes, it retained its formula of being a speedy lightweight, two-seater. By 1970 it was redesigned again and powered by a Ford 1,500cc V4 engine; however, in the USA emission control requirements reduced the performance of the engine so much that, from 1971, a 1,700cc V4 engine was used. This, after emission controls, reduced the power to that of the 1,500cc model at 65bhp. After 1972 US safety regulations also insisted that new low-speed impact proof bumpers were added to cars; these looked completely out of place on the Sonett and changed the characteristics of the original design. As such, Saab USA's president, Jonas Kjellberg, was interested in creating a new generation of Saab Sonett for the US market and contacted Reliant in 1973, aiming to create a deal in which Reliant would design, engineer and assemble the car. For Reliant such a deal would have pushed the work ahead for a new Scimitar GTE building in which the GTE and the Sonett could be built in shifts, side-by-side. This also meant that Saab would have helped to fund the building itself. Reliant contacted Tom Karen at Ogle Design Ltd, who provided concept drawings of a new Sonett whilst Reliant drew up a business plan.

Unfortunately, around the same time, sales of the existing Sonett had slumped following the 1973 oil crisis and Saab announced that production was to end in 1974. Kjellberg presented Reliant's business plan for the new Sonett to the board of Saab Automobile in Sweden, which then rejected the proposals, bringing the whole project to an end.

Employing a fibreglass body, it was planned for a new Saab Sonnet to be built alongside the Scimitar GTE. *Peter Stevens*

Park Place stood directly next to Reliant and, under its ownership, the first house was converted into a surgery for all employees. *Maureen Plant*

Reliant was, at a time, the landlord for the houses at Park Place and used them for storage as they became vacant. *Maureen Plant*

Park Place

Although never mentioned as part of Reliant's history, Park Place was a row of 14 terraced houses that stood next to Reliant on the north side of the A5. Believed to have been originally owned by Tolson's Mill in Fazeley, the houses had been built at the start of the 20th century and were rented to employees of Tolson's Mill and remained as rented accommodation throughout their life span. As detailed earlier in this book, the cellars in the houses provided sanctuary to Reliant workers during air raid attacks in World War 2.

When all 14 houses came up for sale in the late 1960s, Reliant purchased them and took over existing tenants' contracts so it became the landlord until each family moved out. The houses were then used as storage with one of them being filled with Scooter Ski parts. The first house in the row was used as Reliant's surgery. Although the expansion plans for 1972 do not show the houses, they survived until 1977 when they were then demolished to expand further the site on the north side.

Robin 750/Robin 850 (Mk I)

Although the Regal was hugely successful for Reliant with sales continuing to remain healthy, it was starting to age with a profile that had not changed much in a decade. Work on the Regal's replacement — codenamed TW8 — had actually started in 1963 with a model showing similarities to the Robin appearing in a 1967 BBC film detailing Reliant's exports. In the film, Ray Wiggin is shown handling

the model outlining that it was a Reliant car for the future. Eager to create a new updated three-wheeler, Wiggin asked Karen and Crosthwaite to turn their attentions to a possible Regal replacement. Prototypes were then duly created and, in 1971, Wiggin approved and passed this new Reliant three-wheeler for production.

During early October 1973 the first examples of the Robin begun their journey down the new Two Gates production line that had been built as part of Reliant's 1972 expansion project. At the public unveiling of the new car on 30 October, Wiggin announced to the press that, 'This is the car you've all asked for'. Whilst few on the board understood the reason why, the name of the new vehicle came from Roger Musgrave — the Reliant Robin. Following the annual fortnight holiday, workers came back to work to start producing bodies in a totally new fashion with the introduction of hot press moulding. Whilst outer and inner body mouldings continued to be hand laid using traditional techniques, new hot and cold presses were used to make numerous body parts, most notably the doors and bonnet lids.

The Robin was available both as a saloon and a van, and was an entirely new design from the ground up. With Crosthwaite's influence, the chassis was both wider and considerably lighter than that used on the Regal. Ogle's Tom Karen once again put pen to paper to style the Robin's looks and, whilst sharing a similar chassis to the Bond Bug, Karen described the Robin as a 'prettier vehicle than the Bug' with a more rounded and modern shape. There was a reason

Opposite top left: Made in the early 1960s, this 1/8th scale model foresaw the Robin design. Note the potential use of larger wheels filling up the wheel arches. *Tom Karen*

Middle left: A full scale mock-up of the Robin body used for making the production moulds.

Bottom left: One of the rarer colours for the Robin was Carnival Pink, the colour however was not popular and soon dropped from the colour range.

Top right: Introduced in 1973 the R Parts logo on all spare parts helped to differentiate genuine Reliant parts from imitations.

Bottom right: A view of the twin high-level production lines for the Reliant Robin in 1973.

for this; unlike previous three-wheelers produced by Reliant, the Robin was designed in a hope that women (mainly 'housewives and business girls') would take notice of it and perhaps buy one. A range of eight new colours was introduced and Barrie Wills notes that:

> 'One of the launch colours was Carnival Pink, chosen personally by Roger Musgrave, because of his belief he could convert swinging young British 'chicks' to the wonders of three-wheel motoring! Ray [Wiggin] and I were less convinced and when we saw the purchase price of the paint from International Paints, caused by the high cost of the pigment, we quickly made a decision to let Roger prove his point and, if he failed, the colour would be discontinued. That it was, after around six months.'

The Robin was styled essentially to attract people who drove conventional cars as well as motorcycles. For that reason not only was the Robin's interior the most plush of any preceding three-wheeler, its body was very advanced for its time as it was the first vehicle not to have a drip rail running along the body at the top of the doors. Tom Karen recalls that:

> 'Because drip rails were especially ugly on GRP cars (the thickness of the panels being joined there was hard to control) I introduced the idea of hiding it under the door frame. This features on all cars since (I wanted the door shut line to go up against the glass on the A post and into the roof, that would have made moulding easier, but this was vetoed. VW and others did that later).'

In addition, instead of an external boot at the rear, the luggage area was located behind the rear seats with access to it being through the lift-up rear window allowing a loading space of 30cu ft with the rear seats folded down. The Reliant Robin was, therefore, a pioneer of the 'hatchback' craze that then proceeded to sweep through the motor industry, but in 1973 the word was virtually unknown.

The Robin was billed as an 'economy saloon-estate' within its contemporary advertising. Two variants of the Robin saloon and van were offered at the launch, these were the standard Robin priced at £779.35 including VAT (£677.05 for the Robin Van) and the Super Robin priced at £826.42 including VAT (£737.00 for the Super Robin Van). The Super models were different from the standard in that they contained a number of extras; these included a factory fitted radio, cast alloy wheels, heated rear window, spot lights and additional dash clocks. With a top speed of just over 73mph (117km/h) and a claimed 60mpg (4.7-litre/100km), the Robin was powered by Reliant's 32bhp 748cc all-aluminium engine with the four-speed gearbox now having synchromesh on all four gears. Like the Bond Bug, the Robin was also fitted with modern 10in wheels.

By February 1974, just four months after its launch, sales were already heading towards the 6,000 mark with the top-of-the-range

Whilst the Robin was being assembled at the Two Gates site, Robin bodies were created at the Kettlebrook site where a complete body was moulded every 12 minutes.

The official launch of the Robin at Goodwood Race Track in October 1973 also featured a cutaway Robin that displayed the compact layout of the design.

Super Robin accounting for around 60% of the demand. With the Robin being produced flat out and with so little production line capacity available, in May 1974 Reliant halted production of both the Rebel and Bond Bug models to transfer labour to the ever-increasing Robin line. The action it seemed was worth it as, by the end of September 1974, the 10,000th Robin had been sold and the month also saw a new production record, with 330 vehicles a week coming off the assembly line.

The Robin was further endorsed by its connections with royalty when Princess Anne took delivery of a Robin Super Saloon at her home at the Royal Military Academy, Sandhurst in March 1975. Four months later, on 15 July 1975, Her Royal Highness visited Reliant and spent five hours visiting all three sites: Two Gates, Kettlebrook and Shenstone. The Princess had driven herself there in her Reliant Scimitar GTE and, whilst talking to employees, she spoke openly about the Robin Saloon that she also owned.

Left: With the Hodge Group owning 76% of Reliant's shares, this meant that Reliant was also able to offer finance on vehicles via Hodge Finance.

Below: Princess Anne visited Reliant on 15 July 1975 and was given a full tour of all three sites. She is seen here with Ray Wiggin talking to Peter Petricca. For the author the most prominent person in this photo is the chap on the far left with folded arms; this is the author's father-in-law, Barry Mansfield-Stokes, who also worked at Reliant.

This image shows the sheer size of the Robin assembly line with around 15 vehicles just on this particular track alone. *Thomas Touw*

Although the Robin was breaking all records for Reliant, the company was forever looking to the future. In October 1975, the basic 748cc engine was bored out to 848cc and the carburettor changed from a Zenith downdraft to a SU carburettor, increasing power from 32 to 40bhp. This provided a new top speed of 85mph (137km/h) and a 0-60mph (0-96km/h) time of 16 seconds, very respectable for its time. From this point on, the Robin range received an 850 suffix to its name and a few additional tweaks, such as a higher fuel filler, for it had been found that, on 750cc cars, the fuel filler cap had been set too low and in some circumstances, petrol could escape from the cap on sharp corners.

With the UK celebrating the Silver Jubilee of HM Queen Elizabeth II in 1977, Reliant marked the occasion in style with the 'Jubilee' Robin Super 850, of which only 750 were produced. Each vehicle had a special bonnet badge bearing the car's individual number and was painted in Royal Red. The Jubilee also had a silver name style, plus 'Jubilee' insignia etched on the rear window and on the hubs of the alloy rear wheels. The interior was furnished with a silver coach-lining with silver/grey upholstery with matching carpets and headlining. Mechanically there were

The Robin 850 not only boasted, as the name suggest, a more powerful 848cc engine but also a number of more subtle changes like a revised grille that consisted of three chrome bars replacing the former wire type grille.

A number of 850cc engines (denoted by the red top) alongside the Robin assembly line ready to be hoisted up and mounted into a vehicle.

no changes to the standard Robin. The Jubilee Robin went on sale just before the Queen's official jubilee celebrations in the July of 1977 with the batch of 750 being split between 200 dealers. All Jubilee Robins were sold within a few short weeks, with one dealer reporting that he had sold his entire allocation of cars before he'd even finished putting up the promotional posters in the showroom.

Despite the production lines running at full capacity, the Robin received a huge knock in 1977 when it was discovered that, at speed, the steering box could break free from its mounting points thus rendering steering as useless. When discovered, Barrie Wills spent all night doing the arithmetic before asking Ray Wiggin to call an emergency board meeting the following morning. Derek Peck and Dave Rock came up with a solution. All Robins produced at that time were to be recalled for the new bracket to be fitted; the cost was around £1m plus. The board, under Wiggin's direction, made the decision to implement an urgent safety campaign with immediate effect. Each dealer contacted owners that had the affected Robins to return the cars so that a 'strut and cradle' bracket could be fitted; this effectively wedged the steering box against the top chassis rail.

Following the management changes in mid-1977 (detailed later) it is said that the new board, under Ritchie Spencer, failed to continue the campaign with the urgency it required and they were caught out after the consumer protection orientated BBC programme *That's Life* had intervened branding all Robins as potential death traps. In a Christmas letter sent to all employees in 1979 Ritchie Spencer wrote:

> 'Just before closing I ought to mention the TW8 steering bracket; this was a foul and depressing business. I can assure you that we have carried out the procedures laid down in the Government approved "Code of Conduct" for recalls, absolutely to the letter. By the end of the year about 25,000 Robins will have been modified and we shall continue with the recall campaign for as long as it takes to achieve a satisfactory level of success.'

It is often noted that Reliant did not always the latest models in its advertising. Here a 'N'-registered Robin becomes a 'P'-registered Robin 850 for the Robin 850 brochure. The giveaway, however, is the fuel filler cap, which was lower on 750 models.

On its launch Reliant said of the Robin that it had 'a selling life of at least seven years'. Almost on cue, after eight years the Robin (in its present form) was then discontinued in favour of a new three-wheeler for the 1980s: the Reliant Rialto.

FW9

Although initially never an official project, John Crosthwaite started development of a four-wheel Bug; this was planned to be a compact and sporty two-seat coupé that would use the Reliant powertrain. Whilst the concept started as a four-wheel version, Reliant realised that it needed something more innovative to appeal to its customers. Ogle Design worked on the design, making a number of more practical refinements (such as proper doors rather than side screens). Progressing from a clay mock up to a wheeled styling buck in 1973, it used an adapted chassis with the front said to have utilised components from the Rebel. The project was short-lived but it was completed by a Reliant employee who used various Reliant three-wheeler parts.

Restricted to 750 cars, the commemorative 1977 Jubilee Robin sold out in just a few weeks. *Thomas Touw*

The FW9 was designed as a four-wheeled equivalent to the Bond Bug and progressed to a half-finished prototype (pictured) before the project was abandoned.

The Super Helicak was built in Indonesia and based around a revised Bond Bug chassis. *RSSOC*

Development of the FW10 (Kitten) estate is seen here using a modified Robin shell. Whilst the left-hand side of the model rests on blocks of wood, the right-hand side is developed into a four-wheel body and once approved, the left-hand side is then also completed. *Peter Stevens*

Super Helicak

P T Italindo of Jakarta, Indonesia contacted Reliant in May 1973 to ask the company to assist in designing a new lightweight three-wheel taxi to be used in south-east Asia. This was to replace its existing 'Helicak'; this was a three-wheeler based around a Lambretta motorcycle. The 'Super Helicak' was announced in February 1975 although 200 vehicles were already on the streets of Jakarta. Following approval by local city authorities, a further 2,000 sets of components were ordered from Reliant in a deal that was worth £500,000. In collaboration with Italindo, Reliant designed and engineered the chassis; this was based on the Bond Bug chassis and provided in a SKD form. The Super Helicak had a fibreglass body with a steel roof panel from the Mini Clubman Estate, which Reliant purchased from British Leyland, that was designed by P T Italindo. It was powered by an Italian Lawil 125cc two-stroke engine and used a conventional gear shift system with four forward gears and a reverse. The interior had individual front seats for the driver and a passenger and a bench seat in the rear that could seat two adults. A through-flow fresh air ventilation system was also incorporated just beneath the roof to provide fresh air for passengers.

Kitten

With the discontinuation of the Rebel, Reliant no longer had a four-wheel economy car in its line up and so plans were made to design a replacement. Partly because the Rebel had been halted to provide more space for the Robin and partly because the Rebel had a unique body, resulting in fewer economies of scale, it was decided that the new four-wheeler should maximise commonality with the Robin as much as possible. The new vehicle would, therefore, be much cheaper to produce than the Rebel. Ogle Design was then engaged; initially Tom Karen wanted to design a completely different body to the Robin although Reliant wanted to use existing tooling as much as possible. Essentially the front of the Robin had to be redesigned to turn it into a four-wheeler and so Karen set about doing just that, with a prototype Kitten (Code named FW10) being created in April 1975. The prototype, however, looked a bit too much like the Robin with round headlights, a similar wire grille and the same indicators.

Along with slight variances in the body design, the only major visual difference between the two models was that the prototype Kitten had an extra wheel and a wide black bumper attached to the bumper moulding at the front. Ray Wiggin, therefore, went back to Ogle, asking for the design to look a bit less Robin-like. As a result, Karen then modified the front of the Kitten and incorporated rectangular headlamps into a design that was capped by a large black plastic fascia that wrapped around the headlamps. The initial sketch used no grille at all and featured offset vertical slots; this concept was later adopted by Giugiaro in his original design for the basic Fiat Panda. Wiggin, however, did not like this idea and so the grille was redesigned. Only the front end of the Kitten was different

Detailed as the 'car built to stay young', the Kitten was advertised as an ideal town vehicle and 'easy-to-park', Reliant deduced, therefore, that it 'must appeal to women'.

To maximise the economies of scale, the Kitten shared a lot with the Robin and, as such, was seen by many as a four-wheel Robin, looking almost identical from the side doors backwards.

with the vehicle using the same body from the side doors backwards. This meant that both the Robin's saloon and estate bodies could be used. The initial chassis was similar to that used on the Robin at the back though had a redesigned front section to accommodate the extra wheel with the engine being moved forward in the chassis and mounted between the front two wheels. David Raven was taken on as a consultant to oversee the Kitten development programme, with Dave Rock leading the chassis development. His team also designed a Lotus-inspired double-wishbone front suspension. Fitted with Reliant's 848cc engine, like its three wheel counterpart, the Kitten was very economical and able to return up to 60mpg (4.7-litre/100km) at 50mph (80km/h) with a top speed of 80mph. In addition, Reliant heavily publicised the Kitten's turning circle of just 24ft from kerb to kerb — on par with a London taxi.

Exhibited at the Motor Show at Earl's Court in October 1975, the Kitten was on sale two months later as either a saloon model, costing £1449.35 or an Estate version with a price tag of £1,574.82. The saloon version featured the Robin's opening rear hatch whilst the estate version had a single rear door. The interior of the Kitten again resembled the Robin, with many parts being used in both models (though the front had increased space due to the engine being moved forward and, as a result, used a different centre console with an elongated gear stick that came from under the dashboard).

The Kitten assembly line showing both saloon and estate variants.
Thomas Touw

Left: One proposed Ogle design for the FW10 was a pick-up version, though this would have required additional development and tooling for the rear pick-up section. The idea with the Kitten was that it utilised existing Robin body parts as much as possible and so a pick-up version was not pursued. *Peter Stevens*

The Kitten range was increased further, in January 1977, with the introduction of a 6cwt van. With the passenger seat removed the van offered 53cu ft of space or 43cu ft with the passenger seat in situ. Costing £1,508 plus VAT of £120.64, the van was powered by the same 848cc as the rest of the range, with a low-compression engine also available as an alternative. The interior of the Kitten van was similar to the estate version, although the back had a wooden floor that was covered with a rubber mat. At the time the market was starting to be dominated by Japanese vehicles and, as the Kitten van was designed to break into the low-cost commercial vehicle market, every cost-saving possible had to be utilised to make the Kitten van more affordable. One way to do this was to use round headlamps; these were much cheaper units and could be sourced from the Robin parts bin. The Kitten van, therefore, closely resembled the shape or the original prototype.

Sharing so much with the Robin, the Kitten was considered competitive enough to be converted into a left-hand drive version and, under the guidance of Lofty England, exported with the Scimitar GTE to new importers in Belgium, Austria, Holland and Switzerland. In October 1976, a new deluxe version was introduced; this was detailed as the Kitten DL. The DL version moved further away from the Robin with improvements under the body; these included a modified anti-roll bar along with revised springs and dampers and a new interior. The latter included better seats, which now reclined and tilted as in most conventional cars, soft trimmed door casings, additional dashboard instrumentation and, along with a number of cosmetic changes, front and rear fog lights as standard.

Whilst production ceased in 1982, Reliant also sold a number of Kittens in a kit form, providing everything necessary to build a full vehicle. They were also offered to employees at £1,000 each. Although discontinued, the Kitten's chassis continued to be made with minor modifications as, along with the Kitten's running gear, it was now also being used in the Fox.

Left: With a large single opening rear door, the Kitten estate was an ideal car for visiting the seaside offering 35cu ft of load area with the rear seats folded down (11cu ft with seats upright) and up to 60mpg (4.7-litre/100km).

Below: Whilst Reliant stated the Kitten van had round headlights to comply with commercial vehicle standards, the main reason was that they were much cheaper and thus enabled Reliant to set a more competitive price.

Renamed as the Dolphin, the Kitten was manufactured in India by Sipani Automobiles using kits provided by Reliant.

Dolphin

By some form of metamorphosis, the Kitten then became in 1982 the Dolphin although, a year earlier, it had been referred to by Reliant as the 'Indian Kitten' as the rights to manufacture it were sold to Sipani Automobiles in India. Reliant supplied the Kitten to Sipani in a knock down (KD) form, with the first sets of kits heading off to India shortly after the contract was signed in December 1981.

The Dolphin was a standard Kitten but had a few minor changes; these included a new front grille and different wheel trims. As a two-door car, the Dolphin was not that popular as strict restrictions and regulations imposed by the Indian government on two-door cars car meant that it could only be sold in the south of the country. With the launch of the slightly larger four-door Maruti 800 in 1983, which was made by Maruti Suzuki in India, sales of the Dolphin were heavily affected and so Sipani created a five-door version called the Montana. This, however, could not compete with the Maruti 800. In 1985 Sipani had forecast that it would want kits for 1,800 Dolphin cars off Reliant; however, it only bought 425. By 1986 the number of kits dropped even further as Sipani now continued to build the Dolphin manufacturing all components themselves. Production of the Dolphin ceased in 1990 whilst the Montana lasted until 1994.

BRM Engine Project

The chairman and major shareholder of the giant family-owned, Darlaston-based, Owen organisation — Rubery Owen — Sir Alfred Owen and his sons David and John were great supporters of Ray Wiggin's expansion of Reliant during the 1960s and 1970s. Within the Owen organisation was British Racing Motors (BRM), which was headed by Sir Alfred's brother-in-law, Louis Stanley. BRM was best known as winners of the 1962 Formula 1 constructors' championship, with Graham Hill at the wheel.

In the mid-1970s, in a bid to expand its business into original equipment engine manufacture and supply, BRM approached Reliant to offer to develop a high-performance overhead cam version of its all-aluminium engine, at its own cost. It was a 'no-brainer' for Wiggin as it fitted with his long-standing ambition to develop an affordable two-seat sports car, using the Reliant powertrain as its basis.

The project was led by BRM's chief engineer, Peter Windsor-Smith, formerly of Coventry Climax, Daimler and Leyland, who liaised with Reliant's engine development head, Peter Jackson. Windsor-Smith had previously worked in association with Reliant's Deputy Managing Director, Barrie Wills, in all three companies. The project progressed well until the absence of ongoing success in Formula 1, coupled with huge financial losses, led to the Owen organisation ending its financial support for BRM in 1977. The resultant contraction of the independent business, under Louis Stanley's leadership, resulted in the R&D programme coming to an abrupt end, almost co-incidental with Wiggin's departure from Reliant, never to be resurrected. However, one prototype engine is known to remain.

The BRM engine was a high-performance version of the all-aluminium Reliant engine.
Jonathan Heynes

The turning tide

Although Reliant had, for the most part, been fortunate enough to enjoy excellent worker/management relations since its very beginnings, from the late 1960s UK industry as a whole became embroiled in a prolonged and extremely bitter power struggle between the government and the unions, which grew steadily worse as the years went on.

The launch of the Robin had been badly affected in 1973 when the Birmingham Sheet Metal Workers Union called on its members to strike over pay. Many of the workers on the Robin chassis assembly shop were members and so walked out, halting the production of new chassis. A year later Reliant was affected by

industrial action again when, as a result of a coal miners' strike, from 1 January to 7 March, the production of electricity was severely limited. The government decreed that all commercial users of electricity would be limited to three specified days of consumption each week in a bid to preserve existing fuel stocks. In addition, on these specified days workers were prohibited from working longer hours, although senior staff and directors created their own lighting

Available as both a basic model and a more luxurious GLS model that offered several extras, the wedge-shaped Rialto helped to revitalise sales for Reliant.

million and, despite a turnover of £21,648,000, Reliant recorded a trading loss of £899,000 for the 1976/77 financial year. A further loss was recorded for 1977/78 when turnover of £17,469,207 and a loss of £152,639 were posted. During the year 650 workers were laid off, costing the company £600,000 in redundancy payments. By 1979 things were starting to pick up for Reliant and, despite having to recall the Robin for a steering bracket issue and a national engineering strike that badly affected all Reliant's suppliers, the 1978/79 financial year recorded a modest profit of £249,441.

Transported between Two Gates, Shenstone and Kettlebrook on a low loader during the short working hours period of 1974, this large generator kept Reliant up and running, though at considerable expense.
Maureen Plant

Designed by Bertone, the FW11 was initially planned as a replacement for the Anadol and then the Scimitar GTE, though it never reached production. *Onur Selçuk*

by wearing a miner's helmet and lamp wired up to a car battery. Barrie Wills — Reliant's Deputy Managing Director at that time — then located a large second-hand refurbished generator for sale in the West Country for which, after negotiations, Reliant paid an over-inflated price (the owner having a queue of potential purchasers also interested in it).

The generator was attached to a low-loader and shifts were organised as such that the generator was moved up and down the A5 between the Two Gates, Kettlebrook and Shenstone sites in between shifts. This allowed each site to work over a seven-day period with three days of power from the National Grid and four days of power from the generator. Reliant was, therefore, able to maintain and, in some cases, increase its production quota for each week; however, due to the hefty cost of manoeuvring the generator between the sites and paying permitted overtime rates for weekend working, any profit made was eaten away and pushed the company into losses. Full production resumed on 8 March 1974 and the generator was then permanently based at the Shenstone site.

By the mid-1970s, strikes were threatening to paralyse the country and Reliant was not immune as many of its workers were affiliated to the Trade & General Workers Union (TGWU), one of the largest and most militant unions of the era. As a result, the assembly lines were often stationary as the TGWU fought out its national grievances. By 1977, such strikes are believed to have cost Reliant £1

FW11 /SE7

The FW11 was a prototype vehicle that was designed by Marcello Gandini of Gruppo Bertone in 1977 and developed for Otosan in Turkey. It was planned that the FW11 would replace the Anadol. Four prototypes were built, with two of those being sent to Turkey. The car was a modern styled, five-door hatchback. It had a number of luxuries, like electric windows that were not usually associated with European cars at that time. Otosan's parent company, Koç Group, had also been approached by Ford to take over manufacture of the to-be-discontinued Ford Taunus from its Cologne plant and, following Ray Wiggin's departure, Koç Group's chairman, Rahmi Koç — a close business associate of Wiggin's — decided not to adopt the FW11 programme and followed the Ford route instead.

Following Anadol's decision not to build the FW11, Reliant looked into the possibility of replacing the Scimitar GTE with a modified version of the FW11 and so restyled the design further, fitting alloy wheels and a Ford 1,600cc engine. The new prototype was exhibited as the Scimitar SE7 at the 1980 Birmingham Motor Show. Although there were plans for a range of vehicles modelled around the FW11 with engines from 1,300cc to 2,800cc, the design was taken no further by Reliant. It was, however, later refined by Bertone for use by Citroën as the Citroën BX. Two of the FW11 prototypes are still believed to exist.

J F Nash Securities Ltd

Sir Julian Hodge had seen Reliant's turnover leap exponentially from £3 million to £25 million; however, in June 1977, he announced to the Reliant board that, after 15 years, he was regretfully ending his association with Reliant. The main reason behind this was that, in 1973, Hodge Finance had been sold to Standard Chartered Bank for £55 million of which Hodge and his family was said to have collected £14 million. In addition Hodge had remained as a chairman of the Reliant Motor Group and, despite the Standard Chartered's main interest being one of finance, it had stood by Reliant during the double dip recessions from 1973 to 1976. In 1977 the Hodge Group announced that it was going to concentrate on its main financial business and, as such, no longer wished to maintain its industrial interests; the severing of the connection with Reliant was part of that policy. The board at Standard Chartered then elected to sell off 76% of Reliant's shares. Whilst publically Reliant appeared to be cheerful and somewhat optimistically announced that the shares had been purchased by J F Nash Securities Ltd, Barrie Wills reveals quite a different story.

As Hodge had been chosen by Standard Chartered to arrange the sale of Reliant's shares, Ray Wiggin approached him and asked if he could organise a management-led style buyout. With Hodge's agreement that the shares could be purchased at a nominal price per share, Wiggin then started to enlist potential candidates who would join him to help raise the estimated half million pounds that would be required. Initially he asked his colleagues on the board consisting of Barrie Wills (Deputy Managing Director), Roger Musgrave (Marketing Director), Ritchie Spencer (Personnel Director), Mike Smith (Finance Director) and Cyril Burton (Export Director) if they would join him. With the exception of Burton who was somewhat uncertain, everyone else instantly agreed to stand by Wiggin's side. Realising that even more investment was needed, Wiggin approached various contacts within the auto-industry with whom he felt shared his passion for building specialist cars. These included John Barber (ex-Ford, AEI and British Leyland), Donald Healey CBE (ex-Triumph, Donald Healey Motor Co, British Leyland and Jensen), Anthony Good OBE (ex-Jensen) and the potential key investor Joseph Beherman (former British Leyland and Jaguar importer) who, by the summer of 1977, was also eager to invest a considerable amount into Reliant — so much so that he became the de-facto leader of the investment bid.

Back at Reliant, Wills had created a seven-year forward model policy under the watchful eye of Wiggin; this projected a number of new models that could be developed. These included the Wasp, a lightweight two-seat, soft top sports car powered by a Reliant-BRM engine at a price that would position it between the Robin and the Kitten, and a Triumph Stag-inspired variant of the Scimitar GTE that was to be designed, along with a new GTE, by Marcello Gandini at Bertone. Also on the menu was a Dolomite Sprint-type sports car based on the Gandini designed FW11. Furthermore, a deal was also being explored with British Leyland that would enable Reliant to switch from Ford to Rover V8 and Triumph 2-litre engines and transmissions for the larger sports cars. With such proposals before them, Wiggin's new consortium of saviours was very excited indeed about making a bid for Reliant.

With Beherman now being the leader of the bid, Wiggin advised him that using a detailed brief that had been provided by Hodge and offering a price of two pence per share (a total of half a million pounds which, even in the 1970s, was giving the company away) would seal the deal. Much to the horror of the consortium, the bid submitted to Hodge was rejected, not due to the size of the offer but because Beherman was born in Belgium and, therefore, he was 'not British and Standard Chartered wished to see Reliant remain in British hands'.

Just a few days later, Hodge plucked John Nash of J F Nash Securities Ltd seemingly out of thin air, announcing him as the new owner of the Reliant Motor Group. Perhaps a further blow to Wiggin's consortium was that Nash had offered just one-and-a-half pence per share and thus purchased Reliant for £375,000; this gave Nash a controlling interest. Nash was unknown in the motor industry with the only available information on him at the time being his confidence in Ron Atkinson as the manager of Kettering Town Football Club — also owned by Nash. Visiting Reliant, Nash assembled all employees announcing:

'I have studied the forward plans of the Group, which make a lot of sense and show prospects for a bright future. It is my intention that Reliant shall continue to operate with a large degree of autonomy, and I so not envisage any changes in management, structure or general policy.'

Wiggin retained his shares, becoming the second-largest shareholder and, for the press, announced that he welcomed the move, believing that it would allow Reliant to create and exploit further business

a minor boost as mines closed and workers were paid redundancies. Just a month earlier, Reliant celebrated the 10,000th Rialto — a two-door GLS model — to roll off the assembly line, though there was a double celebration as the company also celebrated its 50th Anniversary. A special edition Jubilee Rialto was built to celebrate the occasion. This featured fade out stripes along its body and side indicators. Reverting back to the standard axle, the Jubilee model was only available to dealerships. Like the Jubilee model the Rialto 2 models also switched back to the standard axle ratio and the economy gauge was deleted. Reliant had received numerous customer complaints saying the car had a fault as the gauge always seemed to be reading poor economy, especially when accelerating. With the low-ratio axle, the fourth gear on the Rialto 2 was more of an overdrive and so, if going up a steep hill, it would require a drop from fourth to third gear that was not required on the earlier Rialto. Also whilst the Rialto 2 would do 30mph (48km/h) in fourth gear, unlike its predecessor, it laboured and would not accelerate without a change of gear ... which showed poorly on the economy gauge.

Whilst the Rialto looked a totally different shape to the Robin, they both used the same doors.

The Rialto SE range was introduced in 1986 with one of the more popular models being the estate version. *Thomas Touw*

1985 also saw the introduction of a new low-lead fuel that started to cause problems with the HT-E engine, causing it to pink very badly under load. At the time Reliant released a customer notice saying under no circumstances should unleaded fuel be used in this engine without an additive. Partially as a result, in 1986 Reliant ceased production of the Rialto 2 and reverted back to the Rialto with the standard 848cc engine. After reorganising the entire range, Reliant discontinued all standard variants of the saloon and estate models. This left just the GLS versions of the saloon and estate models in production, both of which were renamed as the Rialto SE range. Contrary to popular belief, the van model also remained in production although it was not advertised as heavily as the saloon and estate variants. The cut backs were not all bad news as, despite several models no longer being promoted, a new Reliant emerged in 1988 in the form of a three-door hatchback Rialto that followed the hatchback trend employed by the rest of the motor industry.

Scimitar GTC

The ideal for an open-top Scimitar had been first initiated in 1976 by Barrie Wills after his appointment as Director of Product Development and Supply. Prior to the J F Nash takeover later in the same year, Wills created a development plan of future models to present to the board and amongst these was a plan to develop a Marcelo Gandini-designed replacement for the GTE with a GTC derivative. In conjunction with British Leyland, these would have been powered by Rover V8 3,500cc engines. The idea was approved by Ray Wiggin though, following the Nash takeover, the plan was then scrapped. Wills' GTC would have been similar to the Triumph Stag that had just ceased production.

With Wiggin's departure and Ritchie Spencer now at the helm, it was instead decided to create a GTC by redeveloping the existing GTE model. Tom Karen at Ogle Design was asked to style an open-top version of the well-established Scimitar GTE. With a number of similarities to the Stag, the new Scimitar had a roll-over hoop for safety reasons and a boot at the rear, along with several other minor changes around the rear lights and vent grilles. Reliant's Ken Wood and his team from the body development department then set about designing the GTC, ensuring the body had additional torsional rigidity to stop the vehicle sagging in the middle. Reliant decided not to manufacture the hood itself and so outsourced it to Coventry Hood & Sidescreen, going to great efforts to ensure that the designed hood matched Ogle's styling. The hood was made from highest quality German Happich material, which replaced a cheaper

The Scimitar GTC may have lost the loading space offered by the GTE though brought back the feel of a traditional open topped sports car.

Although the front of the Scimitar GTC had not really changed from the GTE, the back end now incorporated a new boot.

vinyl that tended to be used in most open-top cars. Internally, the new Scimitar kept its normal seating layout with the rear seats still folding down, providing extra access in the newly designed boot.

The first prototype, codenamed SE8, was finished in 1978 and, after further development, it was in March 1980 that the Scimitar GTC (SE8b) was officially launched. Priced at £11,360, the GTC was almost in a league of its own with only the Mercedes 280SL (costing £6,000 more) as its nearest rival. Continuing to be powered by the Ford 2,792cc engine, the GTC came with power steering, electric windows, electric aerial and Wolfrace wheels that, whilst being on the options list, were pretty much fitted to most vehicles. One of the optional extras for the GTC from 1981 was a fibreglass hardtop that was also fitted with rear screen heater. Unfortunately the GTC did not sell well and even Prince Edward acquiring one for a short time did little to stimulate interest. By 1982 just 20 GTCs were being

built a year before production came to an end in November 1986 at the same time as the last GTE.

One of the main issues with the GTE and GTC was that, following the Nash takeover in 1977, the Scimitar lacked further development and, as a result, did not keep up with its competitors. The Scimitar range was briefly resurrected in 1987 when both the Scimitar GTE and GTC name and design were purchased by Kohli Nakauchi, who was president of the Middlebridge Co. Based in Beeston, Nottingham, a new factory was set up and, based upon an existing Reliant Scimitar SE6B, the company made around 450 modifications to the design. The Middlebridge Scimitar GTE was launched at the 1989 Earl's Court Motor Fair in London and caught the attention of Princess Anne, who ordered a car and was loaned a Middlebridge Scimitar until her car was built. In 1990 the company then went into liquidation with just 77 Middlebridge Scimitars having built.

Although initially created by MEBEA. in Greece, the Fox was then developed further by Reliant, which then went on to use the design itself.

Designed as a replacement for the Scimitar GTE, the SE82 was a slightly larger car designed by Bertone. Despite heavy investment the project was scrapped. *Carl Langridge*

Project SE82

Project SE82 was a possible replacement for the existing Scimitar GTE, the 82 signifying the year Reliant planned to put it into production. In 1978 Reliant contacted the Italian car stylist Bertone to design a new car that was a spacious two+two sports hatch that had a large glass area. The front styling for the new car was approved in January 1979 and Ed Osmond, Reliant's engineering director, travelled to Turin to view a clay model. Slightly longer than the Scimitar GTE (SE6), a full-size mock-up of SE82 was built as was a complete interior, but the project was soon abandoned. It was planned that the SE82 would cost around £15,000 and be powered by a Rover 3.5 litre V8 engine; however, the rising cost of petrol and increased competition in the market from the discounts offered by larger concerns would have made it impossible to sell the car at a competitive price and so Reliant was unlikely to achieve a profit. As a result, Ritchie Spencer took the decision to halt all further development despite spending over £100,000 on the project.

Fox

Reliant exported a number of models and design packages to several companies and countries, one of these being MEBEA in Greece. MEBEA had already assembled the Regal pick-up, TW9 and the Robin under licence and, in the late 1970s, wanted to design and develop a passenger-utility vehicle. This type of vehicle was very popular in Greece as, at the time, the law allowed such cars to incur a reduced tax being rated as commercial vehicles. MEBEA, therefore, modified the Kitten chassis in order to accommodate higher loads and, ultimately, created a prototype of a light utility vehicle with fiberglass body that would become known as the Fox. There was, however, an issue as for MEBEA to manufacture the Fox it would have to obtain a type certification which, for locally designed cars, was particularly convoluted and complex. MEBEA, as a result, approached Reliant, which then developed the Fox further, facilitating the all-important vehicle type approval.

The MEBEA Fox was manufactured in Greece from 1979; however, in 1983, the law favouring such vehicles was changed and, as a result, sales of the Fox plummeted. The model was eventually discontinued after just 3,000 were completed. Rather than abandon the model completely, Reliant decided to use the design for itself for the UK market. The company is said to have spent £500,000 on modifying the Fox; this was based on a slightly modified Kitten chassis, which was galvanised and used Reliant's economy 848cc all-alloy engine. Other changes for the UK included a revised front end, better brakes, larger wheels (now 12in rather than 10in) and a low-ratio axle of 4/1 to improve pulling power, which slightly affected top speed at 78mph (125km/h).

A MEBEA Fox Utility vehicle; this one was shown by Reliant at the 1980 Motor Show at the NEC.

Launched in the UK market in July 1983, Reliant was initially particularly keen to promote the Fox, offering a £50 incentive towards advertising cost to any dealer that used the Fox launch advertisements. With a 7.5cwt load capacity, Reliant advertised the Fox as a 'Multi Purpose Utility Vehicle'. The vehicle consisted of a front fibreglass cab with two seats and had a number of rear options, including a pick-up with a drop down tail gate as well as utility and hardtop versions that came with either a fibreglass top or a canvas cover. In addition, original price lists were quoting an optional removable/fold flat rear seat but Reliant was informed by Customs & Excise of a possible change

Right: Using a revised Kitten chassis, the Fox was essentially a pick-up version of the Kitten; it was available in both hard- and soft-top variants.

Below: Whilst having a great potential, Reliant did not really advertise the Fox as much as other models and as such sales remained relatively low.

to car tax regulations in September 1983. The changes meant that, even if the rear seat was added after the vehicle was purchased, it would be liable for car tax rather than as a commercial vehicle. Reliant, therefore, removed the rear seat as an option and advised all dealers to destroy literature where this was detailed.

By December 1983, the Fox was selling slowly but steadily, allowing Ritchie Spencer to claim that: 'the majority of the people who have bought one and used one are happy with them'. Spencer's plan at this time was to find at least ten major fleet operators (ie: petrol, construction or service companies), along with local authorities, water boards and even the Post Office to help draw in the orders. To help achieve that aim he informed the Sales Department that its main priority for the first six months of 1984 was 'to make a success of the Fox'. The Fox was in a very competitive market and, despite the promising start, sales of the Fox just did not take off and, by the mid-1980s, Reliant advertising on the Fox was kept to a minimum. By 1987, Reliant had all but written it off, forecasting no vehicles to be sold after 1987 although it had found a small market selling Fox bodies in Sweden, where they were being fitted to electric vehicles. Despite this, Relaint soldiered on with the Fox until 1990 when the company went into receivership.

Cipher

With the Scimitar GTE starting to date and become less fashionable, Reliant was starting to look for a replacement for it and was considering a car for the small sports car market. Although Barrie Wills and Derek Peck had rejected an earlier design during the previous year, in 1978 Tony Stevens (a freelance designer) designed a second generation lightweight, open two-seat sports car that he called the Cipher. The vehicle was based on a Reliant Kitten chassis and running gear using the Reliant 848cc engine. The vehicle had a tubular steel space frame mounted to the chassis; this was then covered in separate bolt-on fibreglass panels with a body design that was very reminiscent of the Lotus Elan. Stevens displayed a prototype Cipher at the 1980 Motor Show where it was well received; however, it needed a heavy investment to start producing more cars. Stevens then approached Ritchie Spencer at Reliant with a view to manufacturing the vehicles; Spencer then agreed to build two prototypes for evaluation purposes. Despite the enthusiasm of the

Reliant built two prototype Ciphers; however, it then decided to proceed no further with the project. *Dave Corby*

workforce who created the prototypes, it was worked out by Reliant that actually to develop the Cipher further in order to turn it into a production car would cost in excess of £250,000. Stevens did not have this sort of funding and Reliant was not willing to contribute towards it as they had its eyes set on a Michelotti design (later to become the SS1). With the Scimitar GTE in its minds, Reliant wanted something that could match its performance and so believed the Cipher with the 848cc engine would be underpowered. As a result the company proceeded no further with the project.

Scimitar SS1/SS2/SST

With falling Scimitar GTE sales, Reliant believed that it needed to add a small sports car to its line up and, around the same time, promoted Ed Osmond to be Director of Engineering. Osmond had worked at Triumph on similar projects and with the Italian car designer Giovanni Michelotti, and so Reliant followed Osmond's past experience, turning to Michelotti to design a small sports car. Michelotti had retired through ill-health, but his son, who was running the business, responded with his first design in December 1978. Reliant was considering production when it was approached by Tony Stevens with the Cipher design, as detailed above. After turning Stevens down, Reliant then decided it would use the design styled by Michelotti. Unfortunately Michelotti died in January 1980 before the full finished details were produced, though Reliant decided to continue with the design anyway with Ritchie Spencer and the rest of the board approving the new design. Rather than use a one-piece body shell, Reliant decided to build the new car using a mix of compression, injection-moulded and SMC press-moulded composite panels (that would be less labour intensive than their handlay counterparts) that could easily be bolted on to a backbone chassis. A large percentage of the major panels (ie: front and rear sections, doors and wings) were made by Dunlop using reinforced injection-moulded plastic. The chassis, manufactured in Germany by Thyssen Nothelfer, which part-funded the tooling, consisted of a basic backbone with welded tubular outriggers attached to a central backbone by triangulated pressed steel plates. The suspension was made up of independent rear suspension with coil springs and trailing arms from a Ford Sierra and a double wishbone and coli springs with horizontal telescopic dampers at the front. Power was then to come from a choice of engines, with both Ford 1300cc and 1600cc CVH engines being used with a Ford four-speed gearbox.

The interior of the car was designed by Jevon Thorpe and used many parts that were instantly familiar to Austin Metro and Ford Escort drivers. Internally, only the cockpit structure, steering wheel

Registered in January 1984, FOH 274V was the second Scimitar SS1 prototype built. It is believed to have been written off in 1986 when it overturned at the SCI Road-Going Sports Car Championship.

and cranked gear cover were manufactured by Reliant. With Reliant outsourcing various body panels to Dunlop and, due to its complicated nature, the chassis to Thyssen Nothelfer, when it came to putting all the parts together Reliant faced a number of issues. Firstly, due to the number of different manufacturing processes of the panels, many had different shrinkage tolerances and so were not capable of achieving the panel fits and gaps Reliant planned. Meanwhile the complications in creating the chassis meant that each had slightly different dimensions; this caused issues when trying to attach parts to it. Consequently, there were many problems on the assembly line, increasing both operational cost and the time taken to assemble a car.

The new car was called the Scimitar SS1 (Small Sports 1) and was launched as the 1,300cc SS1 at the 1984 Motor Show at the NEC in Birmingham. Reliant saw the SS1 as a low-cost sports car that offered low insurance rates, perhaps ideal, therefore, for the younger generation, though reactions to the looks of the sports car were divided. Even with uncovered rectangular Porsche 928-style pop-up headlights, Ritchie Spencer admitted with hindsight that the styling at the front of the car was a bit weak and not quite to everyone's taste. He also acknowledged that Reliant spent far too much on developing the SS1; the investment ran into millions of pounds. The looks did put a few people off and, whilst Reliant projected to sell at least 2,000 cars a year, it only sold 500 of them in 1985 and 300 the year after. Whilst, the 1,300cc version of the SS1 was found to be a bit too slow, the 1,600cc version provided better performance, offering a top speed of around 108mph (174km/h) and a 0-60mph (0-96km/h) time of 11.5 seconds.

Opposite top: The wedge shaped nose of the Scimitar SS1 was further achieved with the use of pop-up headlamps that were derived from Triumph TR7 units.

Bottom: Moulded from rubberised deformable plastic, the front nose cone and wings on the Scimitar SS1 were able to resist minor impacts.

Below: Designed by Ed Osmond, the Scimitar SS1 had a complex chassis that consisted of a steel space frame on a fabricated centre tunnel. This then used separate steel armatures front and rear to support the body panels.

The construction of the SS1 proved to be a problem for Reliant as, whilst the vehicle received many criticisms for its looks, there was very little Reliant could actually do about it as the body was made up of numerous, expensively tooled, panels rather than a single-piece body shell, as with the GTE, which allowed more scope for design changes. In addition, with so much of the car being outsourced, long-term contracts had been signed and so they could not easily be changed or cancelled. Reliant was, therefore, stuck producing a car that was expensive to make and, to some observers, somewhat offensive to the eye.

Fitted with a Nissan 1,800cc turbo charged engine, the Scimitar SS1 1800ti even by today's standards was an exceptionally quick sports car offering a 0-60mph (0-96km/h) time of around 7.6 seconds.

In 1985 Reliant offered a hard-top as an optional extra and, whilst it could do nothing with the looks, it could certainly boost performance. This the company did by fitting the Nissan Silvia 1800 Turbo engine. This changed the car dramatically, now giving the SS1 135bhp and a top speed of 126mph (203km/h) and a 0-60mph (0-96km/h) of just 7.6 seconds. Spencer stated that the reason for the delayed introduction of a more powerful SS1 was deliberate, saying Reliant wanted to establish the SS1 as: 'a dream car that most can afford going for volume rather than power first.' Despite the extra power, sales remained low with just 230 sales in 1987, 186 in 1988 and 100 in 1989. From 1986 all models were fitted with a galvanised chassis, increasing the longevity of the car.

One key benefit that occurred as a result of fitting the Nissan unit was that the emissions were lower and so it was able to pass USA emission requirements. Reliant hoped it would be able to sell around 7,000 extra units per year worldwide. Reliant, therefore, planned a strategy to export the SS1 to the USA but the car was still hindered by its looks. Interested in the SS1, General Motors in the USA then commissioned a project to restyle the body for an American version. The task for restyling the SS1 fell on William Towns, who was noted for his Aston Martin designs. It was planned that the American version would be powered by an American 3,100cc V6 engine and so Towns gave the car, now dubbed the SS2, a much more powerful look, with cleaner lines and wider wheel arches. The deal fell through when General Motors withdrew funding and the project was abandoned and so the SS2 design remained unused.

Restyled for the American market, the Scimitar SS2 would have used a much larger engine. The design, however, was not used as the project was abandoned.

With the Scimitar SST, Reliant returned back to fibreglass creating its own body panels rather than outsourcing them.

Undeterred, Reliant used parts of the design, restyling the SS1 to create the SST (T after William Towns). With Ken Wood heading the development team, the SST now employed a one-piece body shell, which was moulded by Reliant and bolted onto the chassis. This made the cockpit more watertight and quieter. Rather than numerous panels like the SS1, the SST had two major sections — front and rear — and so presented much sleeker lines. Engine choices were again provided, though now the 1,300cc engine was replaced with a 1,400cc to complement the more potent 1,600cc and 1,800cc models. The SST was unveiled at the 1989 Motorfair and became available a year later.

Lucas Hybrid

In 1982, years ahead before hybrid vehicles were fashionable, Lucas Chloride EV Systems Ltd in Birmingham contacted Reliant to design, engineer and build an experimental hybrid car. Reliant's electric vehicle links with Lucas went back to the mid-1970s. The car was to be used for research to test the Lucas Hybrid in various modes; this would help determine optimum design parameters for future production vehicles. With a brief that the vehicle needed to be a conventional family-sized car that was powered by both an electric motor and petrol engine, Reliant set to work. Ogle Design Ltd was engaged once more to style a spacious five-door hatchback body; this consisted of a streamlined fibreglass shell fitted with steel side doors. Reliant then worked on the mechanics, creating a new specialised chassis with independent front suspension that incorporated dual wishbones and coil springs, whilst the rear was fitted with leaf springs with a panrod to control lateral movement.

Developed for Lucas Chloride EV Systems Ltd, the Lucas Hybrid was an experimental car that used both an electric motor and the 848cc Reliant engine.

With conventional controls, the Lucas Hybrid was fitted with both a Reliant 848cc engine and a Lucas electric drive generator and could be used in two operating modes. For running during the day, the Lucas Hybrid could (depending on the range) use battery power alone and be plugged into a domestic electricity supply overnight to recharge it. For longer journeys beyond the range of a single charge, a separate auxiliary battery that powered lights, horn, radio etc allowed the petrol engine to be started up to extend the range. Rather than provide drive to the wheels this acted as a generator, charging both the batteries and providing power to the electric drive unit. In addition to this, with disc brakes on the front and drums at the rear, the vehicle also made use of regenerative braking where, pressing the brake pedal, reversed the electric motor thus feeding power back into the batteries.

The Lucas Hybrid made its public debut at the 1982 Motor Show on the Reliant stand and was then passed onto Lucas for testing. Several years later it was then sold and passed through several owners, appearing at the annual Reliant Gathering (initially organised by the author) in Tamworth in September 2007 and 2011. Sadly, since its last appearance, the vehicle suffered damage; it was then broken up into two parts with (at the time of writing) the bulk of the transmission belonging to one person and the main body shell to another.

The assembly line for the Ford RS200 at Reliant's Shenstone plant. Whilst Reliant produced the fibreglass bodies, assembly of the vehicles was supervised by Ford. *RSSOC*

Ford RS200

Whilst Reliant was celebrating its 50th anniversary in 1985, the Ford Motor Co turned to the company not only to produce the body shell for the RS200 rally car but also to assemble it as well. Capable of 150mph (241km/h), the Ford RS200 was a turbocharged, mid-engined two-seat sports car that employed a number of advanced design concepts. These included two- or four-wheel drive that could be selected by the driver. It was powered by a 1.8-litre turbocharged 16-valve, double over-head camshaft, fuel-injected, four-cylinder engine that developed more than 230bhp and could push the car from 0-60mph (0-96km/h) in under five seconds. The body of the car was designed by Filipo Sapino of Ghia in Turin in conjunction with Ford's design groups.

To comply with rally law to ensure the new car could enter the world championships, just 200 of the turbocharged RS200s were built at Reliant's Shenstone plant. The cars were then sold at a retail price of £36,000 each, with priority given to drivers who planned to use them for rallying. Whilst Reliant produced the fibreglass body, Ford provided the chassis and all mechanical components for the vehicles to be assembled and supervised production of the vehicles.

Metrocab

Metro Cammell Weymann (MCW) of Washward Heath in Birmingham was a company well known for building bus bodies. During the early 1980s, Geoff Chater, a taxi engineer from Carbodies (later LTI), and

Bob Parsons (ex-Peugeot-Talbot) worked on recreating the Metrocab taxi concept that had been highly successful in the 1920s with the Beardmore cab that claimed half of the London taxi market. MCW then contacted Reliant in 1987 to design and produce a new fibreglass body for the Metrocab. In anticipation of new legislation that was about to take place, one of the main design points for the body was that it would have wheelchair access, making it the first wheelchair-accessible taxi. The Metrocab used a number of parts from other manufacturers, being fitted with a Ford grille and powered by a 2,496cc Ford Transit engine and a Ford automatic gearbox. Although the vehicle initially had reliability issues, it proved to be more economical than the competition, a fact also noted by *Taxi Magazine*, which noted that, over 36,000 miles, servicing was 16% cheaper than its nearest competitor.

By 1989, MCW's parent company, the Laird Group, ran into difficulties following work with the Channel Tunnel project and was forced it to divest its train, bus and taxi-making interests. Selling off all entities separately, the Metrocab taxi name and design was acquired by Reliant, with full production of the Metrocab being moved to Tamworth. The Reliant Metrocab adopted the same ingredient, though was now powered by a new generation 2,496cc Ford FSD 425 diesel engine with the choice of either a four-speed automatic or heavy-duty five-speed manual gearbox. The fibreglass body was made in sections, so that in a minor collision parts like bumpers, front wings, rear wings, valance panels and doors could all quickly be replaced. As with its predecessor, the vehicle remained wheelchair accessible with large doors that opened to 90 degrees. The body was set low so that wheelchairs could enter the passenger compartment straight from the kerb; where no kerb was available, lightweight ramps were also provided to ease access. Once inside, the wheelchair was locked into place electronically with a retaining belt controlled by the driver.

In January 1990, an angry group of London taxi drivers from the London Metrocab Club, stormed their way into the Reliant plant at Two Gates demanding to know why orders for Metrocab taxis and spares were being met weeks late. The delays meant that some taxi drivers were off the road and so not earning, with one particular driver noted for being off the road 12 weeks. The taxi drivers were suspicious that, despite Reliant acquiring Metrocab, there wasn't actually a production line for it. Their concerns were eased when Alan Bray, Head of Sales and Service, took the taxi drivers to the Kettlebrook site and showed them the production line. He explained that Reliant was having problems acquiring skilled labour to man the new production line and that the company planned to have the line running at full capacity as soon as it could.

Although a very short-lived model, the Reliant Metrocab had a promising start taking Reliant into the taxi market. *Thomas Touw*

No sooner had Reliant started to produce the Metrocab, it ran into problems, mainly due to the fact that the gear ratios of the gearbox were not synchronised with the engine. MCW had traditionally always used a commercial Ford gearbox; however, Reliant had substituted this for one used in the Ford Granada. As a result, numerous faults developed after a few thousand miles. Les Turner, who was at Reliant at that time as a Warranty Assessor, recalls that not many vehicles actually made it through the warranty period without a claim being made. For one customer this was not an issue as 200 Metrocabs were exported to Taxi Combined Services on Sydney, Australia. The vehicles in question were 'gliders' having no engine, gearbox or rear axle. When the vehicles arrived in Sydney they retained the Reliant name and were fitted with General Motors 3.9-litre Holden engines that were designed to run on liquid petroleum gas.

With a price tag of around £17,000, Reliant claimed that the Metrocab was 'the modern taxi for the '90s' and, at its peak, it accounted for 30% of the taxi market in the UK. Unfortunately its life was short-lived as, in 1990, the Reliant Group collapsed. The Metrocab business was then bought out of receivership in 1991 by Hooper, a London coachbuilder which continued to build the cabs in Tamworth until December 2000 when it also suspended trading.

Sale of Reliant South Side

Reliant's footprint was dramatically reduced in 1988 with the sale of its whole south site. Following an Annual General Meeting on 8 March 1988, the board approved an increase in the authorised ordinary share capital for the company from 7 million to 14 million. J F Nash had sought this approval in order to 'pave the way for a possible rights issue or any other issue of shares should the need arise'. Nash also informed the board that the turnover in the second half of 1987 showed that the company needed 'to broaden the base of its activities' if it hoped to survive and that the group needed to look at ways how this could be done. Following an Extraordinary General Meeting that followed, the resolution to this was to sell the south site, which would reduce both Reliant's bank borrowings and operating costs, especially giving falling production figures for its three-wheelers. The board approved the sale of the 20-acre Two Gates south site with a sale price of £1.3 million; this was a major appreciation in value over the £375,000 paid for the entire business in 1977. The sale took place on 3 May 1988 with the land being sold to Gill Menior.

Proposed styling for the PR2 Prototype (MGF Concept car) that was built as a prototype for Austin Rover to evaluate. *Mark Cropper*

Reliant south side seen here in the 1970s; this view with the old mill building remained virtually unchanged for several decades.

With the loss of the whole south site, Reliant now needed to restructure completely the production process across its remaining sites with new assembly lines being created in the Two Gates north site on the opposite side of the A5. As there was no remaining space for the paint shop, this process was relocated to the Kettlebrook plant, where a new paint facility was opened on 10 June 1988 at a cost of £250,000. In total, the reorganisation of the company cost Reliant £400,000. Cyril Burton, now the group's Managing Director (having taken over from Ritchie Spencer who had left to join the Woodhead Group, a year earlier in 1987), optimistically assured Reliant's shareholders that:

'Not only can we maintain present production levels on our Two Gates north and Kettlebrook sites, but we still have scope for expansion.'

The sale of the south side also meant more redundancies. Whilst at its peak Reliant employed 2,500 workers in 1973, by 1988 this had been reduced to 446. Even with the smaller head count, Reliant still remained one of Tamworth largest employers.

PR2 prototype (MGF concept car)

In 1990, as part of Project Phoenix, the Austin Rover Group approached three companies and asked them to produce a prototype for Austin Rover to evaluate. As part of the project, Reliant codenamed it the PR2 prototype (MGF Concept car). Each company was given a design brief that detailed the drivetrain layout and included a fibreglass body shell from an earlier concept car called the F-16 that had been designed by Gerry McGovern. At Reliant, Peter Slater was given the brief to produce a front-engined rear-wheel drive car. Reliant already had its own SS1/SST chassis and so adapted this to fit the body shell by elongating the wheelbase and making the track wider, fitting Austin Maestro front suspension and brakes. The prototype was to use the Rover 3.5-litre fuel-injected V8 engine and so Reliant had to modify considerably the bulkhead so that the engine would fit. Reliant produced two body moulds and a completed fully working prototype, which was delivered within the 27-week deadline given by Austin Rover, Reliant being the only company to deliver on time. Austin Rover tested and evaluated the PR2 prototype and preferred its performance and handling but did not use the Reliant design, essentially because it had rear-wheel drive. Austin Rover mainly manufactured front-wheel drive vehicles and so may have needed to spend additional funds creating a new separate chassis.

The return of the Robin in 1989 with a new design utilising Ford Fiesta headlights.

Robin (Mk II — pre-1991)

By the mid-1980s, the Rialto, whilst still attracting sales, started to look antediluvian when compared to other vehicles on the market and so Reliant decided to create a more luxurious three-wheeler. It also seemed as though the Robin name had engrained itself into society with those unaccustomed to Reliant and its designated model names now calling all Reliant three-wheelers 'Robins'. Whether it was because of this or to recapture the success of the Robin, Reliant reintroduced the Robin model name in 1989. The new Robin, (or Robin Mk II as it is commonly known) essentially followed the same recipe as before, although it now had a new front end. This had a much smaller grille and incorporated headlamps taken from the recently discontinued Ford Fiesta Mk II. In addition both the front and rear featured black ABS bumpers. Offered only as a saloon model, the new Robin LX was mechanically identical to its Rialto

stable mates and emulated the Rialto SE hatchback in terms of styling at the rear. The Robin LX also incorporated a number of new features; these included wrap-around front indicators, reversing lamps and fog lamps that were built into the rear lamp cluster, a new heating system and a remote bonnet release. Added to this were a number of optional extras that included a rear wash and wipe system and integrated front fog lights. Sales of the new Robin were starting to look very healthy; however, no sooner had production hit full speed the company was about to change forever.

It's life, but not as we know it

For its first 55 years, Reliant had remained in business — reaching both the peak of its success and struggling to stay afloat. No matter what was thrown at the company, it managed to survive and soldier on; however, all that was about to change in 1990. Five years earlier, the Nash Group had already determined that it wanted to sell Reliant with Nash wanting to 'rid himself of his charge' given the nosedive the company had appeared to take following its acquisition in 1977. Reliant had, to some degree, managed to stay afloat in these years by selling land and efforts were made to sell the company to both Lotus (then owned by General Motors) and a consortium of American car importers, but Lotus was not interested and a potential deal with the consortium failed. Meanwhile, two property companies (Wiseoak Ltd and Belmont

Homes Ltd) had been set up in 1983 by Carl Turpin and Chris Johnson. By the late 1980s, both companies had become large enough to float on the stock market; however, with the housing market boom starting to stall and house prices starting to fall, both knew that it was not the right time to float the companies on the stock exchange. Following a complicated and expensive 'reverse takeover' in February 1990, 37% of Nash Reliant shares were sold to Turpin and Johnson (who both became directors) with Reliant purchasing both building companies for £16.5 million leaving the house builders in control. Cyril Burton said of the acquisition:

Launched in 1994 the Robin 21 was a limited edition anniversary model celebrating 21 years since the launch of the original Robin.

'In acquiring Wiseoak and Belmont we have brought on companies that are generating the sort of profits we need to pursue our aims.'

Sadly, it was quite the opposite and the financial cracks were now starting to show. An internal memo to the whole board on 19 March 1990 reveals another possible solution to create more cash. The memo was recommending that all the offices at Two Gates were relocated to the Kettlebrook site and detailed:

'The plan has been developed under the assumption that you will understand why the actions are necessary; there being insufficient time to go through the loop of informing you of what you already know.'

Later that month, Reliant publically announced that the company was going to abandon development work on all new models and, instead, the main emphasis would be to concentrate on broadening its business operations. As such, the board asked shareholders' permission to remove the word 'motor' from the company title to become Reliant Group plc. Reliant's idea was that the Reliant Group would be relocated to the Kettlebrook site and that the Two Gates site would be torn down and redeveloped as a housing estate by Wiseoak. The profits therefore would stay within the group.

Reliant applied for planning permission to redevelop the Two Gates site but, despite forecasts that the housing market would pick up again, the bottom suddenly fell out of the housing market triggering a nationwide recession. Reliant knew it was now facing serious financial issues and sold the building companies it had recently purchased for just £1. By June 1990, Reliant announced a pre-tax loss of £4.2 million. This was not only due to the collapse of the property market but also as a result of the Metrocab buy-out along with production set up fees. In addition, Reliant had also invested in a new industrial branch called Reliant Marine. For this Reliant had been approached with a plan to waterproof the Reliant engine and move into motorised surfboards and jet skis.

The debt continued to climb and by September 1990 Reliant's borrowing stood at £5.8 million. Despite every effort and with Reliant Group shares being suspended at an all-time low of £0.03, J F Nash Securities Ltd was declared insolvent. The receivers were called in at 1:30pm on Thursday 25 October 1990, forcing Reliant to cease trading. Touche Ross were then appointed to handle the affairs of Reliant's motor and industrial divisions and, given Reliant's strong order books, was keen to sell Reliant as a going concern. For the company's Metrocab operation, KPMG Peat Marwick McLintock were appointed as receivers. At the time more than 400 people were employed at the company's Two Gates and Kettlebrook sites and 115 employees instantly lost their jobs, though the company's chairman Lord Stokes (formerly chairman of British Leyland) had pleaded with the bankers to allow Reliant to continue trading. Almost immediately interest came from a consortium of Reliant managers headed by Cyril Burton with a management buy-out deal; however, this collapsed in November when further redundancies also occurred. According to the *Tamworth Herald* at the time, the Ford Motor Co was also interested in Reliant, having built up good working relationships, though nothing came of it.

In December 1990, the Metrocab business, along with the Kettlebrook site, was sold to London-based coachbuilders, Hooper & Co, which retained 20 employees. On the same day the Metrocab sell off was completed, the entire workforce at Reliant, some 300 workers, was made redundant just as the staff was about to break up for the Christmas holiday. With the arrival of 1991, the future of Reliant was still in the balance and rumours were rife that Reliant would be sold to an international consortium funded by Sipani Automobiles in India and former Reliant Managing Director Cyril Burton. Such rumours were confirmed in March of the same year when the consortium exchanged contracts with the receivers and a six-figure deposit, believed to have been in the region of £200,000, was paid. Unfortunately a 'last minute hitch' prevented further money from being transferred from abroad and so Touche Ross extended the deadline. By 20 March 1991, the money had still not been transferred to the receivers who then retained the deposit, announcing the deal was over and that Reliant would close if a new buyer was not found. Interest then also came from the Autokam group in Russia who wanted to purchase Reliant and move it lock, stock and barrel to Russia. Autokam planned to discontinue the three-wheeler models and just build a van based on the Kitten; however, this deal also failed when funds could not be moved out of the country into the UK.

Beans Industries Ltd

Reliant's largest creditor was Beans Industries Ltd, which stood to lose a lot of business if the company collapsed. Beans was famous for its Bean car that was made from 1912 to 1932 and the Thunderbolt that broke the World Land Speed Record shortly before the outbreak of World War 2. In later years it became an engineering company and, when Reliant outsourced production of its mechanical parts, Beans manufactured the 850cc engine, gearbox, axle and suspension for the Reliant three-wheeler along with suspension units of the Scimitar sports cars. Beans' manager, Lou O'Toole, initially did not want to buy Reliant; however, following research that indicated there was a market for around 30 Robins a week, he decided to buy it to protect his own business and to revive the Bean marque. Beans bought Reliant in July 1991 for an estimated £1.5 million. Reliant vehicle production restarted under Bean ownership during September 1991 with 90 employees being taken back on at the Tamworth site and 250 at Beans' premises in Tipton, West Midlands. Reliant's offices were also moved to the Tipton site giving Reliant a new West Midlands address which meant that all existing promotional material had to be updated with address labels hiding the previous Tamworth address.

Rialto & Robin (Mk II) — Beans

O'Toole unveiled the first 12 three-wheelers off the production line at Two Gates on 17 September 1991. The three-wheel range consisted of the Rialto SE saloon, estate and van along with the Robin LX, whilst the Rialto SE hatchback had been discarded. Although Reliant had a waiting list of more than 230 would-be-owners, production of three-wheelers now ran at five cars a week produced by a staff of just 15 employees. Both the Rialto and the Robin remained as before; however, visually, once stocks were exhausted, they no longer sported a hatch-type stripe along the skirt of the vehicles. Instead, they had just a single pin stripe down the side, which gave the vehicle a much cleaner appearance.

When the SMMT revised its rules in October 1992 allowing a three-wheeler to be shown at the British International Motor show, Reliant announced a limited edition Robin at the show to mark the occasion. This was launched in 1993 as the LE93. *Alan Gold*

Traditionally, the British International Motor Show has always excluded three-wheelers as they were officially classed as motor tricycles. In October 1992 Reliant made history at the show when the Society of Motor Manufacturers and Traders (SMMT) amended its rules and allowed Reliant to exhibit a three-wheeler in the form of a Robin. To mark the occasion, a special limited edition version of the Robin was announced at the show that appeared in 1993. Labelled the LE93, the model was instantly recognisable with colour flashes that were applied to the sills in either blue with yellow or red with brown on white bodywork with the words 'Ninety Three' just above the passenger (near) side headlamp. Internally, they were like the standard Robin with the exception of an 'upmarket radio cassette player' that was fitted as standard.

In addition to the LE93, a Robin SLX model was launched in the same year; this was initially a limited edition model available in Nightfire Red and Caribbean Blue. Due to its popularity, the SLX remained in production; however, another limited edition was hot on its tracks with the release of the Robin 21 in 1994. The Robin 21 was a 21st birthday model, celebrating the launch of the original Robin in 1973 and was finished in a specially formulated, metallic 'Anniversary Silver' colour with a contrasting blue interior trim. Priced at £7,650, the 21 featured numerous extras, including twin front driving lamps, heated rear window with wash wipe and a cigar lighter along with 'Robin 21' decals on the wings and the rear opening tail gate.

Below: On 8 April 1993 the author was given a tour of Reliant. This was the assembly line at the time with just two Robins on it. During that week, 25 Robins were made with three of those being bound for Austria.

A pair of Scimitar Sabres showing both soft- and hard-top options. *Dave Poole*

Sabre /
Scimitar Sabre — Beans

Keen to get a sports car back into production, Beans took the Scimitar SST and redesigned the bodywork further. This included smoother lines, colour coded bumpers, larger 15in wheels and flared wheel arches, with a prototype being built in 1991. With its new name — Sabre — dipping into Reliant's past, the prototype was unveiled at the Earl's Court Motor Show in October 1991, where it created a great deal of interest. The Sabre was launched in July 1992 and, like its predecessors, was powered by either a Ford 1.4-litre CVH or Nissan 1.8-litre turbo-charged engine. As Beans held a lot of stock, it was able to cut the price, offering the Sabre 1.4 at £11,900, the price being around £3,000 less than its nearest competitor the Mazda MX5. The 1.8 version sold for £14,900. Following a restyle in 1993, the engines were changed to the Rover 1.4-litre K-series and Rover 2.0-litre T-series engines, although the latter was soon dropped, with Reliant returning to the Nissan 1.8-litre turbo engine.

The Scimitar Sabre assembly line; the model was the last sports car built by Reliant.

In 1994 the Sabre was rebadged as the Scimitar Sabre and developed further, with one of the most visual changes being a modified front end with restyled bumpers and lamps. Pleased that the car now truly looked like a small sports car that was pleasing to the eye, the company revealed the redesigned Scimitar Sabre 1.4 at the Geneva Motor Show in 1994. At the show it was an instant hit, attracting considerable European success with Sales Director Stewart Halstead reporting that 18 cars were sold 'straight off the stand'. Sadly for Reliant, the tide had turned and, whilst it had taken the company so long to produce a small sports car that really looked the part, the competition had also been very busy, leaving the Scimitar Sabre up against the odds.

Project R931

Beans was keen to develop the sports car side of the business and, to a certain degree, isolate the Scimitar as a separate 'Scimitar Sports Cars' division. This was most notable in October 1992, when at the Motorshow at the NEC the three-wheelers were branded as Reliant and the announcement of the new Scimitar Sabre 1.4 came under the Scimitar Sports Cars brand. Before the show there was much media speculation that Reliant (or Scimitar Sports Cars) was going to unveil a new sports coupé based on the Fox chassis. Amid much anticipation of the new car, visitors instead were treated to an information pack and a questionnaire on a new 'baby' sports car code named Project R931. Visitors were also shown visuals and asked questions about the specifications of the car. These were said to help decide whether such a car should be put into production.

The design element of R931 was being handled by Fergus Engineering and, with a price tag of under £10,000, the new car was designed to lower the cost of sports car ownership. It would initially be a two-seater, rear-wheel drive design available as either a convertible or a coupé. Reliant planned to use a semi-monocoque steel chassis fitted with a multi-point, fuel injection, catalysed version of its all-alloy 848cc engine; this would be capable of around 95mph (153km/h) with a 0-60mph (0-96km/h) time of around 11.5 seconds. The body concept was based on an original design by Lester Allen Associates and would have used thermoplastic panels. The initial reaction to R931 was said to have been 'strong', although opinions on the new design were very much divided. Plans, however, were suddenly halted due to receivership hitting the company once more.

Project R931's proposed new baby Scimitar sports car.

Reliant/Beans receivership

Following the Beans' take-over of Reliant, things had started to pick up very well and the company was once more moving forward. There was also the possibility of a Russian Reliant when, in September 1992, Reliant announced that the Autokam group in Russia (which had itself made an unsuccessful bid to acquire Reliant a year earlier) might start making versions of Reliant vehicles. It was planned that mechanical parts of the four-wheel Fox would be made in Tipton, shipped to Russia, where the vehicles would be made under licence and then imported by Reliant into the UK. This would have brought the price of the Reliant right down in the UK as it would have been much cheaper to manufacture. Depending upon its success there was a possible similar arrangement for three-wheeler models; however, the deal never came to fruition.

By March 1994, the number of employees at Reliant's Two Gates site had reached three figures again with just over 100 employees. Beans also raised extra revenue by selling off the spare parts side of the business to Unipart. With a short-term financial boost and ample orders to fulfil, it seemed that things were settling down again,; however, fate was again about to deal Reliant a severe blow. Due to debts with some of its subsidiaries and, in particular, one major customer withholding a payment of £100,000, Beans went into receivership in November 1994 with debts of around £2 million, taking Reliant with it. For the second time within a space of a four years, Reliant was up for sale. KPMG Peat Marwick was appointed as receivers and workers were told that redundancies could not be ruled out at a future date. The company continued production at 15 Robins and five Scimitars a week; however, by December 1994, the company was hit by a fresh crisis due to a winter slump in orders. Winter was historically a time when Reliant usually sold half its normal number of cars; however, at this point in time, it announced 28 'unavoidable' redundancies, reducing the workforce to 57. Further redundancies soon followed. Production was then also scaled back to no more than eight Robins and one Sabre a week.

Avonex Group Ltd

With the 'For Sale' signs once again appearing at Reliant, over 250 firms showed an interest in buying Reliant when it was advertised by the receivers. One of these companies was Tewkesbury-based aerospace parts firm, Avonex Group Ltd; however, they faced stiff completion from Tamworth-based property developers, Smiths Brothers. The two companies reached a happy agreement when Smiths Brothers acquired Reliant's Two Gates site and agreed then to lease it to Avonex

(led by Peter Hall), which had brought the Reliant company on 16 January 1995. Avonex paid £250,000 to buy Reliant and paid Smiths Brothers a further £275,000 to lease the factory. Reliant stated that such a move would provide 'a period of stability and the chance to fulfil its potential'. Hall reported to the *Tamworth Trader* (a local free newspaper at that time) that: 'Reliant is a smashing little company and has huge potential. The cars are well made. They are tough, durable and they look absolutely beautiful'.

When asked if Reliant would stay in Tamworth for the foreseeable future, Hall replied: 'Of course it will. Reliant and Tamworth go together like Ferrari and Italy. This company helped put Tamworth on the map.'

By now the Tamworth site had a workforce of 30 employees, which Avonex retained. Financially, a deal was struck up with an international finance house in London; this was contracted to part finance finished cars. This, combined with an overdraft of £150,000 acting as working capital, allowed the production of cars to continue.

Rialto and Robin (Mk II) — Avonex

Avonex continued production of the Rialto and both the Robin LX and LE models and made no real changes to the originals; however, it did change the wheels for larger 12in versions. 1995 also happened to be Reliant's 60th anniversary and so was as good a reason as any to produce a new limited edition model to celebrate the occasion. The new Robin, based on the standard hatchback, was called the Diamond Robin and finished in pearlescent diamond white with grey leather seats. It also featured a stereo radio/cassette with a CD socket and a rear screen washer and wiper.

Whilst the 1995 '850 Pick-Up' was heavily publicised on paper, it did not actually progress beyond a prototype. *Thomas Touw*

An '850 Pick-up' version of the Robin was also created as a result of 'searching through the attic', as Hall put it, and finding plans for the 10cwt Regal pick-up that had been initially designed for the export market. Reliant decided to bring back a pick-up, believing that it could find a market with small businesses and councils. Using a Robin van as a base, the rear section of the roof was removed and a bulkhead was added just behind the front seats. Both mechanically and internally, the vehicle remained the same, using the running gear of the standard models and the same interior. A prototype was built and Reliant were so confident it would go into production that '850 Pick-Up' promotional literature was created and distributed through dealers. Although there was interest in the model, it never progressed beyond the prototype.

During 1995, the remaining members of the Rialto range were finally discontinued, leaving the Robin LX as the sole Reliant three-wheeler in production. A Robin LX van was also made with a hatch and a side-opening door.

Styled by Tom Karen, the Sprint was an attempt to bring back the Bond Bug in 1995. It was far enough advanced to have an official launch date set for 2 April 1996 although Reliant, under the ownership of the Avonex Group, crashed in December 1995 bringing an end to the project.
Thomas Touw

Scimitar Sabre — Avonex

Along with the Robin, Reliant also continued manufacture of the Scimitar Sabre, but only with very limited production at the rate of one car a week. The model remained the same as during the period of Beans' ownership and was built until Avonex itself ran into issues in October 1995. At that point, Reliant ceased manufacturing the Scimitar Sabre and, whilst numerous future plans were attempted to recreate a new sports car with the Scimitar name, the Scimitar Sabre remained the last sports car to be built by Reliant.

Sir Clive Sinclair/Electric Robin

Peter Hall had great plans for Reliant and was keen to expand the range and innovate as the old, successful Reliant had done in the past. Hall, therefore, announced in 1995, plans to produce an electric version of the Reliant Robin. To assist with the project Reliant contacted Sir Clive Sinclair, most notable for his range of Sinclair personal computers in the 1980s and of course the electric, three-wheeled Sinclair C5 that failed to reach the success that was hoped for. Initial plans were created for a vehicle that would cost under £10,000 and could be charged by plugging it into a domestic electricity supply. With a projected range of 60 miles (96km) per charge the car was initially planned for the American market, exporting around 10,000 vehicles a year and taking advantage of new proposed Californian rules for zero-emission cars. A white Robin LX was made that ran on electric power although the project progressed no further.

Sprint

Avonex also had plans to put the Bond Bug back into production, but a quick glance at the Reliant inventory revealed that the entire Bond package, consisting of name, moulds and production rights had been sold by the Official Receivers in 1990 to Mike and Gary Webster of Braishfield, Hampshire. The Websters had been using the moulds to produce three- and four-wheeled versions of the Bug, named the WMC Bug. In order to proceed with its new Bug idea, Reliant negotiated with the Websters with the result that certain aspects of the Bug design were eventually sold back to the Reliant. In mid-1995, Hall contacted Tom Karen, the Bug's original designer, and commissioned him to restyle a Bug for the 1990s with a design that still reflected the original. Karen produced a design that had more than a passing glance of familiarity to the original Bug; however, it was a much curvier vehicle, with frog-eyed headlights, a sunroof and flared wheel arches to the rear. Renaming the car as the Sprint, a prototype was created in bright yellow and the design was completed to such a degree that Reliant announced the new model would be launched on 2 April 1996. Unfortunately, Reliant was yet again to face receivership and so the whole project was shelved.

Reliant/Avonex receivership

Despite Peter Hall's endeavours to salvage Reliant and turn it into a profitable business, within three months of Avonex taking over the company it had already lost £411,000 and by six months was starting to face financial difficulties. Upon acquiring Reliant, Avonex almost immediately had to replenish the component bins as everything had been sold off by the receivers in the past. This, along with necessary start-up costs, immediately ate into the company's working capital and remained a constant issue as components would continue to run out with the result that semi-completed vehicles were then stacked up in the yard, each needing components to complete it before it could be sold. Reliant, therefore, was not bringing much needed cash back into the company. Added to this, although the company was not actually getting completed cars out to dealers, it had increased its workforce from 30 to 110 in just a few months and so staff overheads were also added to the growing costs.

By October 1995, the debt was once more starting to spiral upwards and Avonex did not have the funds to pay suppliers and its work force. Although its situation was confidential at the time, rumours had started to spread amongst Reliant's supplier network with the result that they started to withhold supplies. In December 1995, a London finance group pulled out and, with the non-supply of key components, Reliant had no option than to call in the receivers, Finn Associates. Barely able to gather dust, the 'For Sale' signs were once again up at Reliant.

Reliant Cars Ltd

Finn Associates decided to find a buyer for the whole of Reliant as a going concern. Reducing the workforce from 95 to just 12, limited production was continued to complete the partly-built cars. To help fund this, the receivers were compelled to sell off some key parts to continue cash flow into the production business. The problems at Reliant were becoming main news stories, especially following an advertisement in the *Financial Times* offering the company for sale; this attracted over 60 replies. The first offer came early in January 1996 from Peter Hall, formerly Reliant's director who proposed a Company Voluntary Arrangement (CVA) in which a lump sum would be immediately distributed amongst the creditors and the balance being paid from future profits. After securing backing, a sum of £400,000 was deposited with the receivers on Hall's behalf; if the take-over had progressed, he then planned to restructure the company. The proposal, however, was not successful, possibly because such an agreement took time as it had to be ratified by a judge and the creditors perhaps had more faith in someone not connected with the previous financial situation.

Just after Hall's offer, the receivers were also contacted by Jonathan Heynes, who previously had had a 25-year career at Jaguar providing an in depth all-round knowledge of the auto industry and its suppliers. Visiting Reliant, Heynes found that there were 28 vehicles to complete, although he realised that, once completed, these would technically belong to the London finance house, which had lost about £250,000 during the Avonex period. Heynes approached the London finance house and negotiated a deal in which £100,000 cash would be pumped into the company within the first four weeks so that the remaining cars could be completed. A further deal was then negotiated with the landlord, Smiths Brothers, with a five-year lease at £80,000 per year. In addition, the deal included an optional break clause at two years that would allow Reliant either to purchase the site or to vacate without penalty. Heynes reported that:

'It was clear that the Reliant Company were struggling to continue and the premises in a short period had deteriorated. However, the spirit of the remaining work force remained high and enthusiastic. Also dealers reviewed were also confident of future sales. I visited the Tamworth site on about twenty occasions over the next two months, researching, and reviewing what was required to take over and build Reliant back into a good profitable car company.

'I ensured key personnel would be able to return, Maurice Green Works Director, Brian Benton Production Superintendent, Alan Hunt Machine shop foreman, Roger Dean IT and administration, Mick Hilton service manager, Sid Gray car production foreman and many others who showed great strength of character.'

Another key point for Heynes was to ensure that the supply of components could be continued, this itself being a task, given that Reliant had around 440 suppliers at that time. Following due diligence with its key suppliers, only two suppliers felt they would not be able to continue, whilst those who agreed wanted cash up front before supplies were despatched.

During due diligence, Staffordshire Business Link approached Heynes with a proposal for Reliant to be purchased in conjunction with Fletcher Speedboats in Burntwood, Staffordshire, on the basis both companies used fibreglass and could run in a combined production facility. Following discussions a purchase price of £640,000 for Fletchers (a subsidiary of Hornby plc) was agreed. As administration progressed, another purchase enquiry was received by Finn Associates from an offshore company called Burton West Ltd. The company was part of a large Indian group, San Engineering & Locomotive Co Ltd, which manufactured locomotive engines in Bangalore. San had already purchased the Indian intellectual property rights of the Reliant engine for the Dolphin and so had the commercial rights to produce Reliant engines in India. San had plans to manufacture a small sports car in India powered by the Reliant 848cc engine and so it wanted to purchase Reliant. Finn Associates put San in touch with Heynes and a 50/50 purchase was decided upon with Heynes appointed as sole director. The purchase of Reliant then continued.

Along with this deal, Finn Associates, were working closely with a buyer from an overseas company that was Indonesian-controlled, through a UK agent. This gave Reliant the chance to secure rights for the Indonesian company. These were especially lucrative, as legislation in Indonesia allowed sizeable import duty benefits for importing vehicles from Indonesian-controlled companies. Effectively Reliant had been sold twice, with the overseas intellectual property rights being sold not only to the Indonesian company but also to the UK and Indian manufacturing business, along with the brand name held by Heynes' consortium. Indonesian representatives visited Reliant, obtaining blue prints for the engines, though afterwards nothing else was heard from them.

A week prior to completion of the sale, Finn Associates received another offer, this time from Kevin Leech of Glen Investments in Jersey. Leech was a highly successful businessman having around 60 UK companies in his portfolio and he initially wanted to buy both Reliant and Fletchers outright. Reliant was sold to Jonathan Heynes and then split three ways between Leech, Burton West Ltd, and Heynes — with each paying £450,000. An agreement was reached that Heynes should take control and run the business, with cash flow requirements being split three ways. With the sale concluded, the company name was changed from Reliant Motor Co Ltd to Reliant Cars Ltd and Heynes focused on restarting production. However, he was faced almost immediately with an issue; from earlier investigations Reliant was aware that the engine head and block supplier might be reluctant to supply castings and this was confirmed when an order for 100 sets was refused. The company informed Reliant that Reliant did not own the tooling and, after further investigation, it was found out that they had been illegally purchased by one of the interested parties during the sell-off. Reliant, therefore, instigated an urgent court hearing at the Supreme Court in London in a bid to overthrow the deal, which had been 'incorrectly completed' by the casting supplier. The casting company went into liquidation on the day of the high court trial although the judge ordered that it continue production of 100 sets of castings. Reliant then resourced them; however, the court case had cost the company a six-figure sum which it could not reclaim.

Around the same time, Reliant was contacted by the BBC, requesting to film at the plant for an episode within the 10-part business series entitled *Trouble at the Top*. The BBC proposed that a camera crew would be on site for the first six months during start up. After initial reluctance, Heynes agreed although, for legal reasons, the court case remained confidential within the programme. The 45min programme was shown prior to Christmas 1996 and became a significant turning point. Following the episode, Reliant gained higher exposure, sales increased and suppliers provided credit terms. Heynes notes that the one thing that really helped Reliant at that time was support from dealers.

Under Beans' ownership of Reliant, the spare parts business had been sold to Unipart, which now marketed and controlled all spare parts. As administration had been in place at the time of the sale, Heynes contested the previous contract to be void and along with Leech was able to successfully purchase the complete Unipart stock valued at £250,000. Realising the potential of the high margins to be gained on parts sales, a sub-division of Reliant was created called, 'PartsWorld', which gave Reliant a much-needed second cash flow stream to help fund new model proposals.

Robin Mk II — Reliant Cars Ltd

Reliant's first task was to complete the Robins that had been left semi-completed by Avonex and belonged to the finance company. Within six weeks of production starting, all the finance company cars had been completed and Reliant started work on Robins that had been previously ordered. With increased staff, by week 12, 60 Robins had been completed. Whilst production was starting to increase again, all work was being done using the original tooling and machines that, by now, were really starting to show their age and the moulds were so worn that numerous man hours were being spent on each panel to correct surface ripples. Reliant, therefore, looked to modernise the way it used fibreglass. This, in turn, led to testing chopped fibreglass that was sprayed into the moulds rather than the hand method of layering. Whilst it may have produced body parts quicker, there were concerns about the actual strength of the panels being thinner than before and spraying created more waste and so the new process did not go ahead. As engine and gearbox production was becoming a problem, Reliant then started to obtain major components (ie crankshafts, con rods, pistons, distributors, carburettors etc) from San Engineering & Locomotive Co in India.

Heynes attempted not only to take the Robin slightly more upmarket but also to look at existing warranty issues with the vehicles and correct them by introducing 'quality engineering'. A number of these changes started to appear in 1996 and into 1997. Internally, the Robins had several updates, including new dashboard layout and new instruments, new high-quality Philips radio/cassette sound system, door window regulators, door sealing, strengthened steering column support and increased seat padding. Under the

In 1997 two Robin vans were sold to the US Embassy in London and a special dark Bentley Green van was also made for Princess Anne. Jonathan Heynes (centre), his wife Samantha (opposite on the right) and the Reliant work force mark the occasion. *Jonathan Heynes*

Devoid of wheels, a Robin Mk II body is moved for assembly by means of trolley wheels attached underneath. *Thomas Touw*

bonnet, a new cooling system had been added with an integral expansion reservoir. Externally, along with the introduction of new higher quality paint in seven new colours, the fuel filler had now been recessed and was fitted with a lockable stainless cap. A new rear wash wipe system was also added with a low blade parking position. Optional extras included a stainless steel exhaust system, alloy wheels and a new centre cubby box in leather style trim that fitted in between the front seats. So many changes were introduced at this time that the Robins from this point have been unofficially termed Robin Mk 2.5 by Reliant enthusiasts.

December 1996 saw the introduction of a Racing Green special limited edition that was restricted to 100 cars; this became Reliant's top-of-the range model. As the name suggests, the vehicle was painted racing green with the addition of colour-coded deep pile carpets along with the vinyl on the back of seats being green (rather than grey in the standard model). Other standard extras included RDS radio cassette, fog lights, alloy wheels, chrome door handles, four-branch exhaust manifold (that became an optional extra on other models) and a stainless steel exhaust. A Royale special edition was also released; this was essentially the same specification as the Racing Green edition although was finished in Royale blue with blue carpets and trim and, like the Racing Green model, was priced at £9,654.

August 1997 saw another Robin model with the Robin Clubman Estate LM; this was priced at £6,798.55 and designed as a base model to enable customers to add optional extras to suit their needs. Reliant was also now part of the mobility scheme that enabled disabled people to lease a new car, scooter or powered wheelchair by exchanging their government funded mobility allowance. Reliant created a number of mobility estates that were initially all painted Sherwood Green.

With the arrival of Christmas 1997, the workforce had now been increased to 105 employees and 24 Robins were being built per week. By April 1998, 1,365 Robins and derivatives had been built. Prior to the closure of the Tamworth site, the last few months of 1998 saw a commemorative edition Reliant Robin being produced that marked the last 50 vehicles made in Tamworth. Each one contained a commemorative plaque on the dashboard that stated: 'Reliant Cars Ltd. Reliant Robin Commemorative Edition. No. (#). Built to commemorate the last 50 cars to be built at the Two Gates Factory, in Tamworth, Staffordshire.'

The Supervan name returned in 1997 with a new Supervan 5cwt van that was styled on the Robin Mk II.

Creation of the first Giant pick-up was done by cutting the roof of standard body and then adapting it adding a bulkhead and tail-gate *Thomas Touw*

Supervan/Giant Pick-Up

Reliant returned to the commercial sector in 1997 with the reintroduction of the Reliant Supervan and the Pick-Up. The Supervan now featured a Robin Mk II nose and body built into a 5cwt van form. Like Supervans of old, the rear seat was an optional extra, whilst all other specifications were similar to that of the saloon version. Two versions of the '¼ tonner' Pick-Up were also introduced. The first was the 'Giant Pick-Up' in a basic Giant L version. This was a standard vehicle that used a Rialto nose and had the same load area as the 5cwt van featuring a drop down tailgate. The Giant LX and SLX versions were easily identified, having a Robin Mk II nose and a wider load area that had a side-hinged tailgate that enabled a standard Euro-pallet to be loaded. All models again had similar specifications and interiors to their saloon counterparts.

Plans for the new millennium

Diesel and Reliant EFI engine

Reliant also looked into diesel engines and prepared a prototype diesel three-cylinder Lombardini-engined Robin for evaluation, along with a much noisier Kubota diesel version. Diesel Reliants would have proved satisfactory for emissions and provided outstanding economy and, whilst the prototype gained a positive response from dealers, the project again was not followed up.

Whilst it was believed that all BRM engines had been destroyed (see page 101), Jonathan Heynes was alerted to an engine that had survived and purchased it. Reliant then decided to copy the cylinder head; this was then sent off to San Engineering in Bangalore in conjunction with EFI development, for which San was doing the castings. A standard 848cc engine was fitted with EFI; this was being developed in house by Tim Bishop, who was engineering consultant. The power was much improved, producing 41bhp on the test-bed dyno, and, with emission work and catalyst, would have gone into new four-wheel projects. Reliant also took on Eric Neal from Jaguar, who assisted Bishop and Mirek Staron from Tatra Motive Power. Whilst a prototype engine was designed, no fuel-injected engines were used in production models.

Right: A sketch for a Kitten Mk II for which one development model was built based around the same style as the Robin Mk II. *Jonathan Heynes*

Middle: Hoping to revive the Bond Bug, Reliant started work on a new four-wheel version by adapting a Sprint body shell from 1995. *Thomas Touw*

Bottom: With plans to introduce both closed and open versions, the RFW9 was a new four-wheel Bond Bug that did not progress beyond this prototype. *Jonathan Heynes*

Kitten Mk II/Chassis Cab/ RFW9/Scimitar

Whilst Reliant had desires to introduce larger sports cars, it realised that initially it was better to concentrate on the 850cc models and expand the range. Reliant planned to reintroduce the Kitten; this would now be fitted with either an 848cc EFI MPI engine or a Lombardini diesel. A development model was built using a 1976 Kitten with different front and rear sections but the project progressed no further.

Reliant sold five 'glider cars' that had no engines to a company in Seattle, USA. The cars were then converted and fitted with an electric motor. Reliant, therefore, prepared an electrically-driven Robin at Tamworth. Initially this used a standard gearbox and clutch although a constant-velocity-transmission (CVT) drive was also tested.

Along with the new Kitten, Reliant also intended to create a new four-wheel Bond Bug (codenamed RFW9), again fitted with the 848cc EFI MPI engine. The new Bug would have been available in two versions: a closed-top (Targa) or open Clubman. A four-wheeled Bond Bug prototype was built and showed much promise, gathering a lot of media attention although it also did not reach production.

Also on the agenda were plans for a new chassis cab in which the chassis had been extended by 18in and would be available in various body styles, including a box van. It is believed that these models had issues, both with type approval

The proposed new Scimitar to take the car into the new millennium. The windscreen would have been height adjustable. *Jonathan Heynes*

The last Scimitar, created by Geoff Wardle; this was a full-scale model of a new Scimitar and was 75% completed before the plug was then pulled and the model destroyed. Note the shape of the windscreen outline to be cut out. *Andy Plumb*

and with braking performance; the vehicle would have required large brakes to comply with the additional weight. Prototypes were created, though the vehicle never went into production.

Jonathan Heynes also had great ambitions to build a new small Scimitar 1,000cc sports roadster. Reliant had hoped to restart production of the Scimitar Sabre, though during receivership some of the jigs and moulds for the car had been sold and so tools were not available to make it. It was, therefore, decided it would be better to design and build a new small Scimitar. Several designs were drawn up and development began on a new Scimitar that was a small two-seater with a fibreglass body. The design had a large front grille, which it was proposed would close to reduce drag. The new Scimitar would have also had a shaped windscreen that curved around the driver and passenger whilst dipping in the centre. It was planned that the windscreen would be height adjustable via a mechanical screw. Originally it was envisaged that the new Scimitar would use the 848cc EFI MPI Reliant engine and a Honda six-speed gearbox, which, with a lightweight chassis and body, would have produced around 70bhp. The chassis would have been made from tubular steel with McPherson struts and a live rear axle with a conventional braking system sourced from MG. With the SS1, Reliant had built up a good connection with Nissan and so a Nissan 1,000cc alloy engine was also looked into. A full-size scale model constructed of high-density foam was started by Geoff Wardle, with about 75% of the model being completed; however, the project was halted, marking the end of any future plans Reliant had to reintroduce the Scimitar.

This 1936 chassis from a 7cwt van was part of the vehicle collection Reliant started to collect with plans to open a new Archive Centre at Tamworth; this was, however, never built. *Thomas Touw*

Reliant's north side buildings in 1998 with the announcement of a new housing estate called Scimitar Park to soon take their place.

Reliant also planned to build a new 'Archive Centre' that was to be based at the Tamworth factory and in which Reliant started to re-assemble historical documents, such as original design sketches. In addition, Reliant started to acquire historic vehicles for display; these included a 1936 7cwt van chassis, a 1953 Reliant Regal Mk I and an ex RAF TW9. All vehicles were to have been housed under one roof and the Reliant Archive Centre would have been open to customers, dealers, suppliers and employees.

Tamworth to Burntwood

Things at Reliant were running smoothly and, as arranged, as additional cash was required, the three shareholders were placing working capital into the company in equal amounts by ratio of shares. After the first year, Glen Investments requested a full move from Tamworth to its site in Burntwood and a new lease contract, which paid the rent to Fletchers. San, however, was unsure about the move, believing Reliant should stay in Tamworth as it would be costly and lose several weeks of production. The tenancy break clause after two-years' occupancy with the Smiths Brothers was also looming and meant Reliant could be locked into a further three-year contract if action was not taken swiftly. Whilst Heynes and Leech were keen to purchase the Tamworth site for £800,000, the funds would have been difficult to raise and so the decision was taken to move Reliant to Burntwood.

San Engineering's subsidiary, Burton West Ltd, was concerned about the move and believed its share of Reliant was being diluted and that plans to purchase components from San, essentially due to teething quality issues, were not proceeding as swiftly as it had hoped. After further collaboration, Burton West Ltd sold its share and investment to date to Glen Investments, which resulted in Kevin Leech gaining full control of Reliant. Heynes was then requested to stop further engineering work and to abandon all projects and was informed that everything was to be moved from Tamworth to the new Burntwood site. Leech had personally requested Heynes take the position as chairman; however, Heynes decided to leave, selling his shares to Leech and recouping all his investment and finance input.

With Kevin Leech now in full charge, Reliant, as it had always been known, was to change completely with the announcement that the historical but somewhat neglected Two Gates plant was to be vacated during January 1999. Reliant finally closed its Tamworth doors in December 1998 moving to a brand-new £1,750,000 purpose-built factory at the premises of Fletcher Speedboats in Burntwood, some 15 miles from Tamworth.

Above: Renderings proposing how the Robin Mk III would look. *Andy Plumb*

Left: Adapted from a Robin Mk II master model, this is the full-size clay model of the Robin Mk III that was used for making the production moulds. *Andy Plumb*

Robin (Mk III)

When production of the Robin (Mk II) commenced in 1996 under Jonathan Heynes' leadership, Reliant also looked at the possibility of moving to new Resin Injected Moulding (RIM) techniques and decided to restyle the exterior of the Robin as new body tooling would be required. Whilst the tooling was looked into, a number of new concept ideas for a new Robin were created by Andy Plumb, who had previously designed cars for far eastern royalty directly, before acting as a consultant to Reliant. A Robin Mk II master mould was relocated from Two Gates to Fletcher's site at Burntwood and used as a base for the new design. As part of the exercise, Plumb also instigated an investigation into the use of hemp matting for bodies, as this offered significant strength, weight and cost savings. It was soon discovered that it was not as malleable as fibreglass and could not be moulded into tight corners accurately and reliably. Originally, the new Robin design was going to continue using the Ford Fiesta Mk II headlamps; however, the decision was then made to explore other options. Heynes approved and signed off a new 'more flowing rounded shape' that featured teardrop shaped Vauxhall Corsa headlamps. The whole design process of the Robin took just three months and, although it was only ever referred to as the 'New Robin' by Reliant, it is more commonly known by enthusiasts as the Robin Mk III. There were no prototype vehicles and the production moulds were taken straight from the master pattern, which left no room for error.

The new body shell certainly looked the part and had brought the Reliant three-wheeler firmly back into the modern world. The shape was designed with a plan that all models would eventually have a new family look across the whole range. Every panel was new

Above: The proposed styling for an electric version of the Robin Mk III with the standard front grille removed. *Andy Plumb*

Right: Employing a detachable nose come that covered the Vauxhall Corsa headlights, the Robin Mk III had a much more rounded frontal aspect than its predecessor. *Simon Drake*

Bottom: With the announcement that Reliant would no longer be manufacturing the Robin in 2000, it carried on producing the Robin LX, SLX, and the BRG and Royale (pictured here) models during the run down.

on the Robin. The new model also included new doors and a move back to round wheel arches. Unlike its predecessors, the Robin (Mk III), also utilised a detachable nose cone. Andy Plumb states: 'The nose cone was needed for three reasons:

1. To fit over the lenses of the Corsa lamps with a quality shut gap;
2. For ease of light accident damage repair;
3. For model differentiation and face lifting.'

The new Robin also had bumper graphics that were in the shape of a smile both front and rear to give the Robin some humour. Initially, the plan was that they would be painted in contrasting colour to the main body, although this was an extra process that was deemed unnecessary. The fuel filler was designed to test public reaction and echoed a sporty fuel filler that was designed on the petals of a flower, again adding to the fun nature of the Robin. Reliant was also working on a new interior that included a new dash and door pockets. However, this remained unused with the car retaining a similar interior to that used in previous models. The new Robin (nicknamed 'Teardrop' by the dealers) was launched

at the Burntwood site in March 1999 as the Robin Hatchback. Whilst externally it looked like a new vehicle, under the body it was using essentially the same chassis and mechanics that could be traced back to 1973 and 1975 respectively.

Like its predecessors, the Robin Mk III was again offered in either LX, SLX, Racing Green or Royale form, with prices now ranging between £8,137.00 for the LX and £8,459.00 for the SLX to £9,654.00 for the Racing Green or Royale. The fact that the Reliant three-wheeler made it into the new millennium itself is testimony to brand loyalty by Reliant owners when so many other three-wheeler manufactures had long since fallen

Left: Although the 848cc engine didn't really change that much from the 1975 version, in later models the ancillaries were updated; these changes included, amongst other things, a pre-engaged starter unit.

Below: Along with the Robin hatchback, the Robin Mk III also came in a van version; this was essentially a standard vehicle with the side panels left intact at the rear.

by the wayside. Sadly, by now the Reliant was only really selling to the loyal but ever-decreasing band of die-hard Reliant drivers who would never entertain the thought of driving anything else, rather than to the economy-minded masses and former motorcyclist, which had served the company so well in earlier years.

Reliant was up against stiff opposition as, in 1999, the £10,000 cost of an 848cc Robin Royale could buy the prospective customer almost any four-wheeled 1,100cc to 1,500cc five-door hatchback on the market, and most people did indeed end up choosing the larger car. Furthermore, advances in the car industry had left the Reliant three-wheeler lagging behind in many aspects and even the Reliant's generous fuel economy failed to serve as a selling point as many other cars on the market, both large and small, were now more than capable of matching the Reliant. It was essentially the high purchase price that plagued the Robin from the outset and was an Achilles' Heel that had always set the Reliant three-wheeler at a disadvantage against its competition throughout its long history.

In 2000, it was estimated that there were around 44,000 Reliant vehicles still on the roads and, although Reliant still had orders, it did appear as though the Robin had had its day and on 26 September 2000 Reliant released a press release that stated:

> 'December 2000, will mark the final production date for the manufacturer of the last of the famous three-wheeled Robins to roll of the Reliant production line at Burntwood, Staffordshire. After 65 years of production, the Robin is being phased out to make way for the introduction and manufacture of a totally new four-wheeled vehicle that will be previewed at the forthcoming British International Motorshow at the NEC in October.'

Shortly afterwards it was announced that the new four-wheeler would not be there after all. The author duly went to the Motorshow at the NEC in Birmingham and whilst there, at the Reliant stand there was indeed no sign of a new Reliant four-wheeler or any type of Reliant at all. On show were just a few three-wheeled Piaggio Apes in various forms that included a Pizza Delivery van and an Ice Cream van along with a new Reliant logo on its brochures.

Reliant informed all its dealers that the deadline for orders was 31 November 2000 and, at this point in time, was employing 60 staff on manufacturing, engineering, replacement parts and sales. Always keen to bring out a limited edition model, it was announced that a special limited edition of the Robin called the Robin 65 was to be produced. Restricted to just sixty-five examples and painted in gold, the Robin 65 had a walnut dashboard, leather upholstery, alloy

Built to mark the 65th anniversary of the Reliant Motor Company, the Robin 65 was the last model built by Reliant with the final car leaving the factory on 14 February 2001. *Thomas Touw*

wheels, stainless steel exhaust, chrome door handles, special paint finish, driving lamps, white instrument pack and RDS radio/cassette all as standard, within a price tag of £10,000. To make each vehicle unique, each had a numbered plaque that was engraved with the original owner's name. Although December 2000 was the initial deadline for all production, not all orders had been fulfilled and so production continued into 2001 with the final Reliant Robin 65 rolling off the production line on 14 February 2001 (which actually now marked 66 years and not 65). The last Robin 65 was purchased by the *Sun* newspaper, which had held a nationwide competition in September 2000 to name the colour of Del Boy's van in the BBC-TV series *Only Fools and Horses*. The winner was John Leigh of Weaverham, Cheshire, who then went to the Reliant factory to collect the car although, due to space restrictions, Reliant requested that there was no media presence.

Type Approval

Behind the scenes, Reliant also had issues with type approval on some of its models. In later years many vehicles were incorrectly registered with the Driver Vehicle Licensing Agency (DVLA) as Robins or Rialtos with many owners asking why the paperwork for their Reliant actually detailed a different model to what they had purchased. It has been stated that the Giant Pick-Up versions were often registered as vans whilst the Robin Mk III, being quite different to earlier models, apparently did not have the necessary Certificate of Approval to allow it to be sold in the United Kingdom or the rest of Europe. They were registered as earlier Robin LX or SLX models. The Robin Mk III was designed to pass Type Approval test and used a Robin Mk II as a starting point, as Type Approval and 'Grandfather rights' meant that changing things like glass and door hinges was impossible. As such, it is said that Reliant did not declare and certify the design. For the Robin, the regulations boiled down to 'projections' legislation (radii and lamp heights and viewing angles) so this was taken into account with the Robin Mk III, bearing in mind there were to be no prototypes. The Vehicle Certification Agency (VCA) had become aware of Reliant's new models and was pursuing the company, providing it with an option to either gain the necessary certificates or cease production. This issue, combined with falling sales, resulted in Reliant choosing the latter.

Built by San Motors, both the San Storm (seen here) and a saloon version, the San Streak, were for a short while models offered by Reliant.

Halfway between a car and a Scooter, the Ligier 'BE UP' was just one of a small range of vehicles imported and sold by Reliant.

Piaggio/Ligier/San Motor

Abandoning vehicle production completely, Reliant now concentrated all its efforts on the UK sales of Piaggio and Ligier vehicles from France, for which it had been appointed import agents during 1998. The Piaggio Ape was a three-wheeler available in various forms whilst the Ligier was available as a small microcar. Reliant found a small market for the Piaggios with a number of companies. Sold alongside the Reliant until production ceased, with prices starting at £2,675 for a

Piaggio Ape van and £4,995 for a Ligier Ambra, both were much cheaper than the standard Reliant at £8,137. Once the Robin ceased to be manufactured, Reliant expanded the range of imported vehicles; this now included a Piaggio truck and a mini-bus and continued to sell them until 2002. In 1998, Reliant also distributed promotional material for the San Streak and the San Storm, a small saloon and a sports car built by its shareholder San Motors India Ltd. The models were dropped later in the same year when San's subsidiary, Burton West Ltd, sold its share to Glen Investments.

B&N Plastics Ltd — Robin BN-1/BN-2

To all intents and purposes it seemed as though the Reliant story was over; however, no sooner had newspapers proclaimed that the Reliant Robin was no more, there was renewed hope a few weeks later as it was announced that the car was back again. Les Collier of B&N Plastics Ltd, of Sudbury, Suffolk, believed there was still a market for the Reliant three-wheeler and so he approached Reliant Cars Ltd with a view to purchasing the production rights to the Reliant Robin Mk III. Reliant was more than happy to oblige and, in March 2001, after Collier paid £25,000 that was underwritten under the government's Guaranteed Loan Scheme, announcements were being made that the Robin was back under the new name of Robin BN-1. Initially the vehicle was to be called Robin BNP (BNP for B&N Plastics) though this was soon changed to BN-1 when parallels were made between the name and the political British National Party.

Reliant itself announced the return of the Robin with this 2001 advertisement for the Robin BN-1.

Right: The final assembly stages of the first Robin BN-1 in May 2001; this car was then used as a test vehicle. *Les Collier*

Right: One of three Robin BN-1s that were shown at the official launch on 12 July 2001 at Grays of Thrapston in Northampton.

Under the assumption that all certificates of conformity were up to date, Reliant was contracted to B&N Plastics Ltd. to supply five complete sets of rolling chassis and all the parts including consumables for £4,400 per set per week, less the body. However, B&N reported that it did not receive even one complete set. Under the agreement, B&N Plastics collected all the moulds and tooling from Reliant so that B&N could manufacture all the fibreglass and vacuumed parts. Due to a number of issues with the moulds and tooling with certain parts not fitting as they should, Collier used the opportunity to include a number of improvements that distinguished the Robin BN-1 from the former Reliant version. Whilst outwardly, the BN-1 looked identical to past Robins manufactured by Reliant, internally there were a number of modifications; these included changes that Reliant had planned, but did not use, such as a brand-new dashboard design — something that had not essentially changed since the first Robin in 1973 — along with a wider rear seat, increased sound proofing, new door casings and a sunroof fitted as standard equipment. Mechanically the BN-1 also had a slightly modified gearbox and axle. The progress and development of the first vehicles was catalogued online with the author being the official webmaster for B&N Plastics. The first completed vehicle was a silver prototype finished in June 2001 and was then kept as a test vehicle.

Whilst B&N Plastics built the bodies and assembled the vehicles, the chassis and running gear were provided by Reliant. *Les Collier*

Whilst a Robin BN-1 nears completion, several others in the background await their turn.
Thomas Touw

The Robin BN-1 was officially launched on 12 July 2001 at Grays of Thrapston in Northampton, a Reliant dealer. Three Robin BN-1s were present, with one being the silver prototype and the others the first two production models priced at £9,995. At the same time, also almost hidden away on a desk in the corner of the showroom, were several A4 leaflets detailing a more luxurious variant that was soon to be produced called the Robin BN-2 with price tag of £10,800. This was fitted with electric windows as standard and finished in a 'light-reactive' paint, which changed colour when seen from different viewpoints.

The new Robins had created much interest with the story also being picked up by newspapers and TV stations and by the launch date, B&N Plastics had received 132 orders. It was initially planned for a limited production of 250 vehicles to be built a year; this also included plans for an electric-powered Robin that would have a range of 50 miles between charges and a top speed of 50-55mph (80-88km/h). The jubilation of the launch was short-lived as the media attention caught the eye of the Vehicle Certification Agency (VCA), which telephoned Collier, informing him that no vehicles should be sold or manufactured until the appropriate test had been carried out by the agency and Certificates of Conformity were issued. Reporting the phone call back to Reliant, Collier discovered the Robin Mk III did not have the certificates, though Stewart Halstead at Reliant offered to pay for them, believing that they would only take a few weeks to arrange. The VCA did not share the same view and, until the certificates were in place, this effectively rendered it illegal to sell the BN-1 until such modifications had been made. Les Collier and his

company worked solidly for six months to gain the certificates but, during that time, cash was flowing out with nothing coming in, taking B&N Plastics towards receivership. After appealing to the Secretary of State to save both his business and workforce, production was able to recommence on 21 December 2001.

With production now up and running, as 2002 was ushered in, it seemed as though things were now starting to pick up; however, a further blow was to hit Collier. A new bank manager had been assigned to the B&N account and, as the new manager did not see the project as favourably as his predecessor, debts were called in, putting further strain on the business. Reliant also wanted paying and, although it never did follow it through, allegedly threatened court action for non-payment. As Reliant components dried up and the debt continued to climb, Collier had no other option but to close the factory down. In October 2002, B&N Plastics Ltd made the following announcement:

'Despite trying our best to produce the Robin BN-1/BN-2, things have not been going too well for us recently. There are many rumours about what has happened and that we have finished but we have not bitten the dust yet and still intend to somehow continue producing this vehicle sometime in the near future. At the moment our future is solely dependent on gaining financial backing to help us continue keeping this great British vehicle alive.'

Unfortunately no financial assistance arrived and the Reliant three-wheeler finally came to an end. In total, 18 vehicles were manufactured by B&N Plastics consisting of 13 Robin BN-1s and five Robin BN-2s. Following closure in late 2002, a part-finished car from B&N Plastics was sold in 2008 to Eddie Kelly of Northern Ireland. Kelly completed the vehicle using all brand-new and authentic parts allowing the car to retain its 'new' status. As such the vehicle was registered as a new vehicle on 29 April 2009 and today remains the last Reliant three-wheeler to be registered as a brand-new car, seven years after the end of production.

Reliant PartsWorld Ltd

In October 2002, with the dotcom bubble bursting, Kevin Leech went bankrupt virtually overnight as his investments collapsed. Reliant then ceased trading and its subsidiary Reliant PartsWorld was passed over to Stewart Halstead, who then moved the operation to Cannock in Staffordshire. Headed by Halstead the company still exists at time of writing and offers replacement parts and reconditioned engines for Reliant economy vehicles.

Scimitar Park and other sites

Reliant remained on the north side of Watling Street until 1998. The land had been sold during receivership in 1995 to Smiths Brothers who leased it back to Reliant until 1998. When Reliant vacated the site, Smiths hoped to renovate it and lease it to small engineering companies; however, the land was then purchased by Beazer Homes with the Reliant buildings being demolished in February 2000. In its place a new housing estate was erected with a series of 81 one-, two-, three- and four-bedroomed homes. In acknowledgment to its heritage, the new estate was called 'Scimitar Park' with the main road leading into it being named after Reliant's founder as 'Tom Williams Way'. Three other streets adjoining this were all named after Reliant vehicles with Regal Close, Robin Close and Fox Close. The last-named perhaps the strangest of choices, given it was not one of Reliant's most successful models and initially designed for export.

On the south side of Watling Street, where Reliant was actually founded, the land was sold to a company called Probus Creative Housewares in 1988 and the Reliant buildings knocked down a year later. Probus then moved to an alternative site in Tamworth in 2000, the land was sold again to McLean Homes Midland Ltd and a new housing estate of 170 homes was built. The names of the streets were dedicated to the retrieval of parts from an Enigma machine from a sinking German submarine during World War 2, which helped to crack encrypted codes including the Enigma code. One of the people involved was Able Seaman Colin Grazier from Tamworth, who, along with Lieutenant Tony Fasson, lost their lives retrieving the codes. The streets include Grazier Avenue, Bletchley Drive, Petard Close and Fasson Close amongst others. Fasson Close itself almost circles the land that housed the original Reliant buildings from the 1930s.

In its later years, the fibreglass moulding plant at Basin Lane in Kettlebrook had been used to build the Metrocab from 1989 and was sold with the Metrocab business in 1991 following the collapse of the Reliant Motor Group. Metrocab continued to use the site until 2003 when it moved to other premises near Polesworth. The site was sold to Lovell and, following the demolition of the old buildings, 115 houses and apartments were built. The main road was an extension of Basin Lane and so retained its name, though an additional road was created and named Barlow Avenue after Samuel Barlow who started a coal business in the canal basin (hence Basin Lane) in 1870.

The machine factory at Shenstone was sold in 1990 with the collapse of the Reliant Group though it had been cleared of all engineering machinery in 1981 when all engine production was moved back to Tamworth. The premises were then used as a storage facility and the cobwebs dusted off in 1985 for assembling the Ford RS200. The building continues to exist and still serves as an industrial unit.

A 1969 Scimitar GTE seen here in Tom Williams Way with Robin Close off to the left, Regal Close to the right and Fox Close at the top. *Dave Poole*

Reliant Production Figures

Approximate figures for all UK production vehicles. This list covers a primary model type so (for example) the production figure for Regal Mk VI will include both van and saloon variants. For the early years especially precise production figures for models are not always available and so the figure has been worked out based on chassis numbers (although many early 1935 models had no chassis number stamped). In later years production figures are further complicated with Reliant often registering Rialto models as Robins and Robin Mk III models registered the same as the Robin Mk II.

Three-Wheelers

7cwt (JAP engine):	171
10cwt (JAP engine):	528
8cwt (Austin 7 engine):	487
12cwt (Austin 7 engine):	42
8cwt (Reliant engine):	2,026+*
12cwt (Reliant engine):	459+*
Regent 10cwt:	3,225
6cwt:	1,247
Prince Regent:	252
Regal Mk I (TW1):	340+
Regal Mk II (TW2):	1,330+
Regal Mk III (TW3):	4,702
Regal Mk IV (TW4):	1,695
Regal Mk V (TW5):	5,041
Regal Mk VI (TW6):	11,530
Regal Mk VI-A (TW6a):	500
Regal 3/25 (TW7) & 3/30 (TW7a):	105,824
TW9:	1,888
Bond Bug (TW11):	2,268
Robin Mk I (TW8):	27,641
Rialto (TW8a):	15,039
Robin Mk II (TW8b) & Mk III	7,218
Robin BN-1:	13
Robin BN-2:	5

Economy Cars

Rebel (FW4):	3,500
Kitten (FW10):	4,551
Fox (FW10a):	601

Sports Cars

Sabra:	333
Sabre (SE1):	44
Sabre Six (SE2):	77
Scimitar GT SE4 (Straight Six):	297
Scimitar GT SE4a (3 litre V6):	539
Scimitar GT SE4b (3 Litre V6):	51
Scimitar GT SE4C (2.5 Litre V6):	118
Scimitar GTE SE5:	2,469
Scimitar GTE SE5a:	6,635
Scimitar GTE SE6:	543
Scimitar GTE SE6a:	3,877
Scimitar GTE SE6b:	437
Scimitar GTC SE8b:	442
Scimitar SS1 (Various engines):	1,057
Scimitar SST:	45
Sabre Mk1:	39
Sabre Mk1.5 (seem to be a mix of SST and Sabre parts):	20
'Scimitar' Sabre Mk2:	100**
Middlebridge Scimitar GTE:	79
Middlebridge GTC:	1
Approximate total of Reliant vehicles:	**220,501**

*Production figures are not known for 1939 – 1940

** 91 Built, 9 unfinished/ unregistered

Powered by Reliant

When Reliant started to install its new OHV light-alloy engine in vehicles from 1962, it also opened up a new side-line for Reliant selling the engine to a number of companies for use in their own products. The list below details just a few companies that have found a use for the Reliant engine and a few examples as to how the engine has been used.

Allett Lawnmowers — Allett started buying engines from Reliant in 1966 and used various engines from 600cc to 850cc as the engines were changed. The Allett lawnmower was, at the time, claimed to be the world's most powerful and sophisticated motor mower. They were also the only mowers in the world to be powered by a four-cylinder engine with a four-speed and reverse gearbox. The best mowing speed was said to be 8mph (13km/h) although the machines could move much faster than that. Like the Scimitar GTE, the Allett also has royal connections as, for a number of years, two of them were used to cut the grass at Windsor Castle.

Angus Fire Armour — The 850cc engine was chosen in 1977 to be used as the basis of a lightweight fire pump designed primarily for use by fire brigades. The size meant it was small enough to fit the standard fire appliance locker whilst its light weight meant that it could be mounted into a pump and the easily manhandled by two adults. An optional trailer unit was also designed to carry the pump and all necessary equipment.

An Angus Lightweight 1200 Super portable pump built around an 850cc Reliant engine.

Panther — The Reliant engine has also acted as an outboard power unit when a number of 850cc engines were purchased in 1976 to power Panther inland waterway cruising craft. The engine and battery were housed in a fibreglass cover and then 'marinised' by means of converting the engine to power a propeller under the water. Compared with standard marine engines the Reliant unit was said to be quieter and have less vibration.

Powermaker International — The Reliant engine was also used to save lives, when in 1975, Powermaker International started to buy 750cc engines from the company to build generators that were easily manoeuvrable. These were kept on standby at hospitals and patients' homes ready to power kidney machines for patients suffering rare kidney diseases in the event of a mains power failure. Each engine was housed in a canopy and mounted on a trolley and provided 12 hours of power before it needed refuelling.

Quasar — The Quasar was a semi-enclosed feet forward type motorcycle built from 1975 that was powered by a Reliant 850cc engine. Able to exceed speeds of 100mph (161km/h) the engine was enclosed within the body of the vehicle.

Wildcat — The Wildcat was a machine created in 1972 that used the Reliant 700cc engine to provide a legal speed of 12mph (19km/h) although it was capable of 18mph (29km/h). It was created for off-road use with a 17in ground clearance and large low pressure tyres. It was capable of climbing or descending 40° slopes and enabled the user uninterrupted shooting or fishing. The interior was designed to ease entry from a wheelchair and the vehicle was driven by hand controls. The machines were mainly sold in the USA.

Reliant Derivatives

Although outside the scope of this book, the Reliant chassis and powertrain have also formed the basis of many other vehicles with many of the companies involved contacting Reliant directly. The list below details just a few companies that have used Reliant running gear.

Asquith Motor Carriage Co Ltd — Originally a reproduction furniture business, the Asquith Motor Carriage Co Ltd was formed in July 1981. Based in Great Yeldham, Essex the company created hand-built replica vintage vans with a 1920s theme and, in 1986, produced the Shetland van that used a Fox chassis and running gear. Asquith contacted Reliant and the latter is believed to have supplied around 40 chassis complete with powertrains. With cast aluminium, artillery-like wheels the vans certainly looked the part and a number were purchased by companies for use in mobile advertising.

Debono Coaches Ltd – In 1985 an open back utility vehicle known as the Comino was built in Malta by Debono Coaches Ltd. Using a fibreglass body, the car used the chassis, running gear and instrumentation from the Fox that was provided by Reliant. Few vehicles were built.

Leige — Designed by Peter Davis, the Leige is a lightweight two-seater influenced by sports cars of the 1950s. It was designed and developed between 1985 and 1996 in Bidford-on-Avon, Warwickshire, and uses a fibreglass body with an integral floor bonded in. Whilst early vehicles used a modified Robin rear axle, later vehicles used a live rear axle from a Bedford/Suzuki Carry. Power was provided by a Reliant 850cc engine that also retained the Reliant gearbox. In 1996, Davis was in talks with Reliant, hoping for the possibility that the Leige would be produced as a 'turn-key' product. Reliant, however, did not take on the project and so the car was sold in a kit form with customers expected to find their own Reliant parts. Around 60 kits were produced between 1997 and 2005.

PK Manufacturing Ltd —The PK Jimp was a small utility type vehicle designed by Peter Kukla and built by PK Manufacturing Ltd of Sandbach, Cheshire from 1981 to 1984. The vehicles were based around a Kitten Chassis (though some also used the Fox chassis) and used the Reliant 850cc engine and running gear. Using aluminium body shells, the Jimp was available as a 'turn-key' product or as a self-assembly kit car. It is believed that 67 Jimps were made; these ranged from an open pick-up, pick-up with canvas tilt, hard-back van and an open top.

Built upon a Fox chassis and running gear, the Shetland van was styled with a 1920s theme complete with cast aluminium artillery like wheels.

Despite hopes that Reliant would produce the Leige as a turn-key product, it declined and so the vehicle was available in kit form. *Thomas Touw*

Reef Engineering — In 1977, John Crosthwaite started his own company called Reef Engineering and started to build and export open-top cars for tourists at holiday resorts in the West Indies and the Seychelles. Based in Atherstone, Warwickshire, Crosthwaite purchased a number of Reliant Kitten chassis and power plants from Reliant and mounted an open body that was styled by Peter Bailey. The vehicles were called Cubs with one of the first orders seeing 50 Cubs being shipped to Avis in the Seychelles as hire vehicles.

Ricketts — This was a Reliant dealer in Streatham. In 1972 it created the Gilcolt, which was based on a Reliant Regal chassis and running gear. It had a fibreglass body, which was enhanced by gull-wing doors either side of an extended nose. The Gilcolt was sold in both kit form and as a complete car although no more than four vehicles are believed to have been made.

Salamander — Commissioned by the Salford & Manchester Social Services (SALaMANder), the Salamander was produced from 1981 and designed as a replacement for the soon to be withdrawn 'Invacars'. The vehicle was built on a modified Kitten chassis and powered by a Ford 1,100cc engine with a C3 automatic gearbox. The two-seat fibreglass body slightly resembled that of the Kitten from the front and was well specified, with power assisted brakes, electric windows and a tailgate release. It was also designed with easy access doors and allowed a wheelchair to be loaded into the rear hatch. It was built until 1984 when the mobility scheme,

Shipped to the West Indies and the Seychelles, the Reef Cub was essentially an open-top Kitten.

The Tandy Fox was a two-berth motor caravan conversion created by Tandy Industries using a Fox.

started a few years earlier, started to gather pace and rendered such vehicles obsolete.

Tandy Industries Ltd — Based on the Isle of Wight, Tandy Industries Ltd designed and built a motorhome around the Fox. Built from 1984, the conversion of the Fox into a motorhome came in two varieties: the Firecrest and the Goldcrest. The latter had a higher specification, which included a refrigerator, a third berth, catalytic heater and a full oven. Whilst the prototype was built on the Isle of Wight, subsequent production was moved to Portsmouth on cost grounds. Production continued until 1986 with 50 Fox motorhomes being built.

Tempest Cars — Styled as a lightweight classic style two-seat roadster, the Tempest was originally designed by John Box and Ian Foster. The prototype was launched in 1987 and was based around a Fox chassis complete with Reliant 850cc engine and running gear.

In addition to this, every other mechanical item, including the heater and dash instruments, was also supplied by Reliant. The Tempest was available 85% finished and supplied with all components necessary to complete the vehicle. Around 24 vehicles were built when production was hit in 1990 when Reliant went into receivership. As the supply of new parts dried up, the Tempest was then only available as a kit for converting a Kitten or Fox. The rights to the Tempest were acquired in 2000 by Stephen Campbell, of Sportsman Ltd, and then, in 2006, by John Melody, who added a number of upgrades to the original design. Tempest Cars was sold again in 2011 to Joe Mason and is now back in production using a Fox or a Kitten as a donor car.

Whilst the Tempest was in production in the 1980s, John Box also developed and built a 1930s styled van called the Vantique; this was again based on the Fox chassis and running gear. Following the

The Tempest roadster and the Vantique van. Joe Mason

prototype in 1989, just 11 vans were built with 10 of these being completed by 1993. The Vantique also used the only four Fox chassis that were built by Beans after it acquired Reliant following receivership.

Trident Motors Inc — In late 1982 brothers Roger and Denny Vincent of Trident Motors Inc (a division of KVV Enterprises) located in Columbus, Ohio, USA, contacted Reliant with a view to using the Rialto chassis and running gear in their own vehicle, the Trident R-834. After visiting Reliant, a contract was signed in December 1982 for Reliant to supply rolling chassis in KD form. Fitted with Reliant's 848cc engine, the Trident R-834 range included a number of utility vehicles. With a steel body and an enclosed cabin that had seating for two, each Trident had a 1,000lb payload capacity dump bed with a hydraulic tilting system and a 'quick pin disconnect system' that allowed components to be interchanged from various models. Early models of the Trident R-834 had a single headlight. However, in 1985 the vehicles received a number of changes; these included dual headlights with indicators mounted either side. Reliant continued to supply chassis up until the late 1980s when production of the vehicles ceased.

Zoe Motors Inc — In 1983 Zoe Motors Inc contacted Reliant with a plan to introduce the Reliant Rialto to the American market. Based in California, USA, Zoe was a marketing and distribution company formed by James McPherson and over the years they imported various three-wheelers and microcars to the USA selling them under the Zoe brand. Reliant agreed to supply standard left hand drive Rialtos which then had restyled interiors fitted by Zoe to cater for the American market. Introduced in 1985, the standard model was sold as a Zoe Z/5000 with a price tag of $5,300 and with the exception of new badges and paint work remained unchanged on the outside though had a new interior that consisted of a restyled dashboard, air conditioning and leather seats. Due to disappointing sales, Zoe then attempted to make the Zoe Z/5000 more appealing later in the same year with the Zoe Z/3000 ST. This version was modified further with the rear axle and bodywork being considerably widened along with new suspension. Although extensively marketed, with both 'sedan /wagon' and 'panel van' variations offered and costing less than $6,000, only six Z/3000ST prototypes were built, of which three are believed to exist today.

Using a Rialto chassis and running gear, the Trident R-834 was a utility vehicle built in the USA.

Bibliography

Commercial Motor: Various editions 1935-1955

John Z, The DeLorean & Me: Barrie Wills (2015)

Reliant brochures & publications: Various 1936 – 2002

Reliant internal documents: Various 1975 – 1990

Reliant Review: Various editions 1961 – 1977

Reliant Three Wheelers: John Wilson-Hall (2014)

Rebel without Applause: Daniel Lockton (2003)

Tamworth Herald: Various editions - 1935 – 1998

Tamworth Times: Various editions – 1990 – 1995

The Birmingham Post: 1963

The Reliant Three-Wheeler 1935-1973: Stuart Cyphus & Elvis
        Payne (2011)

The Reliant Three-Wheeler 1973-2002: Elvis Payne & Stuart
        Cyphus (2012)

The Scimitar and its forebears (Second Edition): Don Pither (1990)

Websites for Further Information on Reliant (all websites are
available at time of print):

Author's Reliant Website: www.reliant.website

Author's Three-Wheeler Website: www.3-wheelers.com

Dave Poole's Sporting Reliants website: www.sportingreliants.com

Reliant Kitten Register: www.kitreg.org.uk

Reliant Motor Club: www.reliantclub.co.uk

Reliant Owners Club: www.reliantownersclub.com

Reliant PartsWorld: www.reliantpartsworld.co.uk

Reliant Sabre and Scimitar Owners Club: www.scimitarweb.co.uk

Reliant Spares: www.reliantspares.com

Reliant Spares Online: www.chgperformance.co.uk

Index

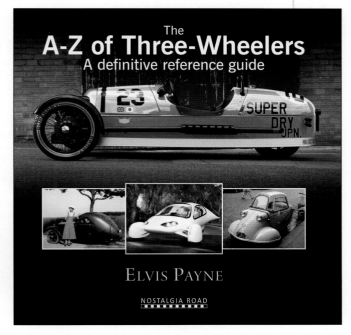

The A-Z of Three-Wheelers

A definitive reference guide since 1769

Elvis Payne

- ■ Comprehensive coverage of over 400 manufacturers and 1000 models
- ■ Early steam, petrol, diesel, natural gas, electric, solar and air powered vehicles
- ■ Includes cars and trucks and invalid carriages
- ■ Over 450 photographs many rare and unseen
- ■ Introduction by Charles Morgan

Love them or loathe them the 3-wheeler, Cycle-car or even Tri-car, has had an important impact in the development of the present day motor car. From the beginnings of the Industrial Revolution to the Concept cars of the future, these vehicles can hold their headlamps up with pride. They were present at the birth of motoring and possibly may be the answer to the future with the constant depletion of the Earth's energy resources.

The first self-propelled vehicle in the world was a steam powered 3-wheeler developed by Frenchman Nicolas-Joseph Cugnot in 1769 with, over a century later in 1885, a Benz 3-wheeler being the first recognised machine to be powered by a gasoline engine.

From pioneering machines such as John Knight's 1896 Petroleum Tricycle and Nazi scientist Count S. von Teleki's WWII Bubble Puppy to the modern sporting vehicles of Razor Cars and the iconic Morgan 3 wheeler, this fascinating chronicle covers over 1000 models from more than 400 manufacturers.

Vehicles from such varied manufacturers as Allard Clipper, Brütsch, Heinkel, Singer and Zundapp, combine with the innovative 1933 Dymaxion built streamlined 3-wheeler, Daihatsu delivery trucks, the 1938 USA built Trimobile and Reliant's much-loved Robin to bring to light the story of hundreds of remarkable 3-wheeled vehicles.

Organised by manufacturer including full details of all models and over 450 photographs, together with an introduction by Charles Morgan of the Morgan Motor Company, *The A-Z of Three-Wheelers* is a comprehensive guide to this classic mode of transport.

ISBN: 978 190834 7169
272 pages, hardback, 250mm x 250mm
Over 450 photographs
Price: £21.95

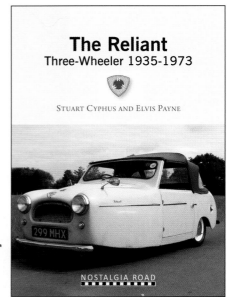

The Reliant Three Wheeler 1935-1973

Stuart Cyphus and Elvis Payne

■ Includes 5cwt -12cwt, Regent, Prince Regent, Regal and Bond Bug

■ Detailed history of Reliant's cars and vans

■ Details of Two Strokes special versions

Founded in 1935 by T. L. Williams in Tamworth, the Reliant Motor Company produced three-wheeler vehicles that met the need for an economical form of motoring.

During the company's heyday, it provided the motorcyclist with a whole new means of transporting the family in comfort whilst its commercial range of vehicles served everyone from the local butcher to the largest of organisations.

Reliant began producing the humble three-wheeler van powered by JAP and Austin 7 engines in the 1930s followed by girder fork vans using its own side-valve engine in the 1940s and 1950s.

The Regal range introduced a new 5cwt version of the van and the 1950s saw the development of the side-valve range to be followed by overhead-valve variants powered by Reliant's aluminium engine in the 1960s and 1970s. The Regal 16cwt pickup and the TW9 three-wheelers were made both for the export and later the domestic market. The company was also responsible for the iconic wedge-shaped Bond Bug, manufactured by Reliant but bearing the Bond name.

Special versions of the Regal — the TS Safari and the TS GT produced by Two Strokes Ltd — complete the history of the first 40 years of this iconic British motor manufacturer.

ISBN: 9 781908 347022
64 pages, paperback, 210mm x 148mm
Over 80 b&w photographs and 20 images
Price: £7.95

The Reliant Three Wheeler 1973-2002

Stuart Cyphus & Elvis Payne

■ Completes the Reliant three wheeler story

■ Exclusive chapter by Jonathan Heynes, owner 1996 – 1998

■ Covers the TW9, Bond Bug, Robin 750, Robin 850, Rialto, Rialto 2, Robin (Mk II), Sprint, 850 Pickup, Giant, Diesel prototype, Robin (Mk III), Robin BN1, Robin BN2

1973 heralded perhaps the most iconic Reliant of all, the Reliant Robin. Built on new assembly lines, production was so rapid that the Bond Bug was halted as the Robin swallowed up additional factory space. With its new 750cc OHV engine the Robin set new levels of comfort for the Reliant 3-wheeler and was soon uprated with an 850cc engine. New commemorative Jubilee and GBS models of the Robin also appeared.

The 1980s saw the wedge shaped Reliant Rialto emerge with a Rialto 2 hot on his tracks fitted with a HT-E engine. The Robin name came to the forefront again a decade later when it was re-introduced with the LE Ninety Three and Diamond special editions.

A new Bond Bug – The Sprint – emerged in the 1990's but failed to make production. Reliant were now struggling to survive despite numerous take-overs and former owner Jonathan Heynes describes his time with Reliant between 1996 and 1998 just before the stylish Mk 3 Robin was introduced to take Reliant into the new millennium.

ISBN: 9 781908 347060
64 pages, paperback, 210mm x 148mm
Over 80 b&w photographs and 20 images
Price: £7.95